£2.49
CW00701513

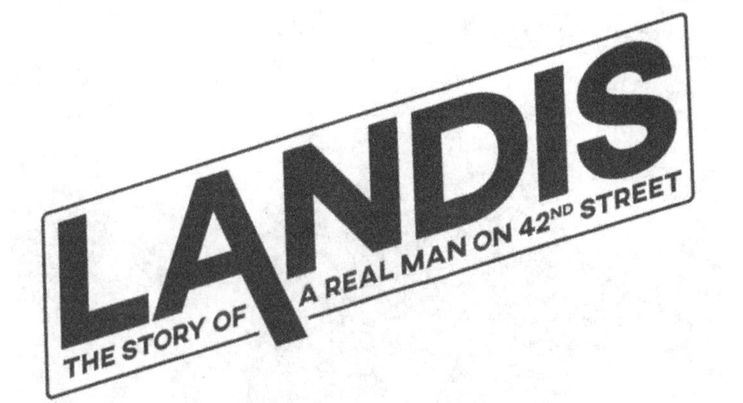

written by

Preston Fassel

Bill Landis, 2005. Photo by / used with the permission from Carl Abrahamsson

Cover Photo by Jamie-Summers Ettinger,
courtesy Art Ettinger

Copyright © 2021 Preston Fassel.
All Rights Reserved.

Portions of this book originally appeared on
dailygrindhouse.com

No part of this book may be reproduced in any form or by any electronic or mechanical means, including information storage and retrieval systems, without permission in writing from the publisher, except by a reviewer who may quote brief passages in a review.

Encyclopocalypse Publications
www.encyclopocalypse.com

Daily Grindhouse
dailygrindhouse.com

PRAISE FOR PRESTON FASSEL'S
THE DESPICABLE FANTASIES OF QUENTIN SERGENOV

'Fassel is a double threat of insane imagination and graceful command of storytelling. Quentin's tale is heartbreaking, relatable, and seriously out of this world.'

Ahlissa Eichhorn, FANGORIA

'... strange, weird and heartfelt in the best of possible ways... Fassel's work is quickly defining its own singular voice in genre fiction.'

John Palisano, Bram Stoker Award-Winning author of *Ghost Heart*, President of The Horror Writers Association

'...part Wolverine origin story, part Darren Aronofsky sports drama on ecstasy, with a generous sprinkling of Kafka's "Metamorphosis"...Yes, it is bananas at times... but bananas in a delightfully fun way.'

Rebecca Rowland, Ginger Nuts of Horror

'...an absolutely bonkers thrill-ride through the heyday of professional wrestling and bizarro fiction... a ridiculous page-turner that both surprised and delighted me! Buckle up, because Quentin is a wild ride... secret Nazi experiments, professional wrestling, and gore galore. What more could you want?!'

Jeff Heimbuch, Horror Buzz

'I love everything about it... a nonstop thrill ride. It's so crazy-- but in a good way. Fassel has a way with developing both relatable characters and story you can't get enough of.'

Jennifer Bonges, Pop Horror

'...gloriously, over-the-top insane. It's also a hell of a lot of fun...Tammy and the T-Rex by way of John Waters with a dash of Tusk for good measure...'

Michael Patrick Hicks

'I didn't know I needed a book about wrestlers, Nazis, twisted love, and dinosaurs, but thank goodness it exists... readers will quickly sink into this bizarre reality, eagerly soaking up the vivid descriptions and unsavory characters until the final moments.'

Nico Bell

PRAISE FOR PRESTON FASSEL'S
OUR LADY OF THE INFERNO

'One of the ten best horror books of 2018.'

Bloody Disgusting

'...a delicious piece of grindhouse literature stocked with strong characters, a vivid sense of place, and real, raw emotion.'

Cemetery Dance Magazine

'Fassel's writing, quite simply, is spectacular... like a fiery lighthouse beam pinning me to the page.'

Herman Raucher, author of *Summer of '42*

'Fully rich and deep, Fassel's characters leap off the page with colorful descriptions. Never sentimental, the hope and agony is robust and palpable…'

Barbara Crampton, actor and producer

'Written with grace, restraint and poise, the prose is evocative, at times almost poetic; edgy when it needs to be, sometimes suggestive...And when the horror does take place, its detail is measured and carefully crafted.'

Isobel Blackthorn, author of The Drago Tree

'...the final showdown is a fitting knockdown, drag-out battle between two of the toughest broads in the Big Apple. If you've ever felt the '80s needed more chicks that kicked ass, Inferno has them in spades.'

Rue Morgue Magazine

'...reminiscent of a 70s grindhouse style, using transgressive violence to elevate and illuminate... fantastic and will leave your gut churning.'

Rebekah McKendry, Ph. D., Shock Waves Podcast

'...well-paced, full of intimate detail, and so unlike anything I've ever read that I can't help but give it my highest recommendation...'

Izzy Lee, *Diabolique*

OTHER BOOKS BY PRESTON FASSEL

Our Lady of the Inferno
The Despicable Fantasies of Quentin Sergenov

For Kayleigh, my Agrippina, who cut down the obstacles in my path and helped me carry Bill into the light.

Table of Contents

A picture you won't ever forget because it touches the full spectrum of the bizarre, the forbidden, the twilight areas of a life destined to be spent in shadow and agony. The screen may never again relate to this subject matter. It will certainly never again approach this treatment... The only ones left to mourn, the last witnesses to the execution; suspended in time by a puppeteer with blood on his hands. Little dolls that go on dancing after the music has stopped...".

Ad copy, Three on a Meathook

INTRODUCTION

Ghosts of Times Square

The dead speak but we as a people
have forgotten how to listen.
Patti Smith

It's a sweaty autumn afternoon in a motel in Nyack, and there's a panic in the air. It's 1985, the tail end of the Golden Age of Pornography; video has supplanted film as the genre's preferred medium and the shoulder-mounted camcorders are humming. Production values, storytelling, and trappings of arthouse legitimacy have given way to quick, cheap thrills. Now, the name of the game is loosely plotted, inexpensive smut shot on the fly to create the minimal viable product— reasonably attractive people fucking to climax with a clear enough a focus to satisfy the indiscriminate horndogs who'll be buying the VHS tapes for $60 bucks a pop in some florescent-lit nightmare Times Square sex shop, the kind of place where the customers wear trench coats and knee-socks even in July.

The problem today: that all important climax is critically missing. Maybe it's nerves; maybe it's inexperience; maybe it's too high a dose of the party drug of the day— ubiquitous, omnipresent cocaine, heaped around porn sets like mountains of Alpine snow free for the snorting— but the male star of the hour is unable to perform. His sequence has already been shot; stubble-beards are being stroked, moist foreheads dabbed. Thousands of dollars are riding on the ability of an overly-muscled, overly-narcotized man to blow his load for all of perverted posterity. The clock is ticking. Our leading man can't be counted on any longer.

It's time to call in the ringer.

Out of the shadows steps a man short in stature and swarthy of complexion. He looks boyish in comparison to his fellow costars; doffing the oversized plastic sunglasses that swallow the upper portion of his face, his eyes bulge in manic anticipation of what's about to transpire. In short order his shirt, jeans, and undergarments have joined the glasses on the floor in a costume change worthy of an oversexed Clark Kent. He is eager; he is willing; he is ready; and he is more than capable.

He is a man of many talents: writer; ethnographer; critic; historian; porn star; IT guy. His name today is Bobby Spector; he writes under the name Mr. Sleazoid;

he was born Bill Landis. He is twenty-six years old and he is one of the New York porn industry's premier stunt cocks. When the man on the video box can't finish the job, Bobby can— he has been in over a dozen pornographic films since 1982 and he has come in every one of them. Over the course of the next thirty-five years, he will add husband, father, trailblazer, influencer, and grindhouse icon to his curriculum vitae.

Today is his day. He will perform the scene admirably; hugs will be given, high-fives accepted. Tonight, he will return to his apartment on 14th, write a critical essay on a recent popular horror film, and spend the rest of the evening in a cocaine and heroin stupor. Before the decade is over, he will codify an entirely new school of cinematic journalism. In another two decades, he will write one of the definitive texts on exploitation film criticism. Before he's fifty, he'll be dead.

*　　　　*　　　　*　　　　*　　　　*

Bill Landis is a ghost.

He haunts not just the fabled 42nd Street that he chronicled at both its apex and nadir but the halls of genre journalism itself. His spirit manifests itself in fragments— a cautious mention here as a source of unlikely inspiration, a shuddering anecdote there, starring him as a malign presence whose malice still looms large over the lives of those survivors of the Deuce still left alive to tell the tale.

He haunts me. It was his book *Sleazoid Express*—

written with his wife, collaborator, and muse Michelle Clifford— that gave me my first introduction to grindhouse cinema, peeling back the curtain on an entire subgenre of film and subculture of filmgoers that continues to influence and impact me as a creator almost two decades after I first entered Bill's realm. For a teenager growing up in rural Oklahoma, in a small town still inhabiting the Reagan age sixteen years after it ended, Bill and Michelle's words were nothing short of a revelation. I'd rented *Heartbreak Motel*— the more artistically minded, less rape-fueled producer's cut of *Poor Pretty Eddie*— sight unseen and was both scandalized and fascinated by what I'd just watched. Where had it come from? What did it mean? Those were the questioned I wanted answered when I Googled the film one frozen Oklahoma day in 2004. Among the first hits I got was an Amazon link to Simon and Schuster's *Sleazoid Express: A mind Twisting Tour Through the Grindhouse Cinema of Times Square*. I eagerly ordered the book, and I was not disappointed. It was the window into a forbidden world every adolescent growing up in one of America's lost backwaters dreams of. I was no longer in Oklahoma; I was on The Deuce, inhabiting an entire ecosystem of the damned that felt more familiar and comforting to me than my Rockwellian surroundings. Bill Landis made me. Without his writing, I would have no bylines, no books, no awards. There would be no *Our Lady of the Inferno*, no *Fangoria*, no *me*. I owe my life's trajectory to Bill Landis; and when I finally went to offer him my thanks, he was already dead. Since his death in 2008, I have tried to learn about the man who set me on my life's path. Especially in the internet age, we can be so profoundly touched and guided by those we never meet; I wanted to know about the flesh and blood human behind the words responsible for where I'd ended up.

But Bill Landis is a ghost.

There is no comprehensive biography of him. In the wake of his passing he left behind a scant IMDB bio, a few obituaries of the sincere and sarcastic variety, an extensive pornographic filmography, and a body of work that remains largely out of print for reasons that have as much to do with the legal as they do with the esoteric. The vast majority of his friends, enemies, acquaintances, and cohorts predeceased him; more leave us every year. He inhabited and encapsulated an era defined by a live-fast, die-young ethos that would astound Joplin and Hendrix. So I decided to chase the ghost— to follow it down the neon-drenched ruins of the Times Square he loved, through the scattered remnants of his own writing, into the memories of the few surviving compatriots he left behind. For years, I struggled in vain to track down those who loved, hated, or simply just knew him; few would talk, even fewer on the record. He'd left behind a complicated legacy, and for fear of speaking ill of the dead, no one wanted to discuss their time with Bill Landis. In a dark irony, the COVID-19 pandemic would prove to be the breakthrough his story needed: the death of exploitation legend Joel Reed sent shockwaves through the grindhouse old guard. One of the last remaining legends of the Deuce was gone, and the other survivors were suddenly eager to make sure their stories of that time got to live on, regardless of the warts. People were eager to talk to me now, and, what's more, they were eager to give me leads on others who could help me tell Bill's story. Years of research suddenly came to fruition, and from the bleak confines of quarantine, I began at last to assemble the tale of Bill's life.

In that lost, damned, golden age we call the 80s, there was a porn star named Bobby Spector and a writer named Mr. Sleazoid. Most importantly of all, there was a man named Bill Landis. This is his story.

1. BILL

The writer must be a participant in the scene... like a film director who writes his own scripts, does his own camera work, and somehow manages to film himself in action, as the protagonist or at least the main character.

Hunter S. Thompson

William Zachary "Bill" Landis was born in France on May 21st, 1959; his father, Zachary Landis, a WWII veteran, was serving as a master sergeant in the United States Air Force at Landes de Bussac airfield. An only child, his closest generational cohort was his cousin Patti Pallidin, of Johnny Thunders fame. Although it's unclear whether his father's being stationed there was intentional or a request inspired by filial piety, it was the very region that gave the family its surname. "Landes is the Euro spelling-- like Corleone in the

Godfather movies" Landis would recall to *Creeping Flesh* contributor Jan Bruun. What little information about his childhood is available is focalized through Landis' own heavily negative and traumatized lens. He would write about it in perfunctory detail only later in life, in "Body for Rent: A Journey Through the Ruins of the Porno-Chic Empire," a heartrending article published in the December 12, 1995 issue of *Village Voice,* after a decade of chronicling the misery and degradation of those around him with precious little comment on the circumstances that had made him so at home in the Times Square criminal underworld. He described his father as veteran of "numerous Far East bloodbaths," his mother as a prescription pill addict content in her addiction because— like so many housewives of the 1950s who were encouraged to blindly accept their doctors' advice— her abuse was medically approved.

Following his birth, Bill's family found themselves transferred to England, where he spent the first five years of life in the Douglas Club— today, the Lancaster Gate Hotel— a "home-style service" residence catering to the families of Air Force veterans stationed in the UK. Despite the invective with which Landis would recall his childhood, it's easy to read between the lines and see a story not unfamiliar to many a Boomer born to Greatest Generation parents: a distant, PTSD riddled father who buried the horrors of war beneath copious amounts of booze; a codependent, enabler mother who looked the other way on her husband's crippling mental affliction while self-medicating with, per Landis, a combination of prescription pills and martinis.

Between one parent unable to cope with his own personal trauma and another unable to recognize it, Landis found himself, from an early age, tasked with caring for both of them. "My father the sergeant would lie on the bed and command me to 'take care of it,'" Landis later recalled of his mother's dinner table blackouts. "I felt loyal to my country because I did my job correctly and precisely." As his own coping mechanism, Landis found escape in the cinema— specifically, the *James Bond* franchise, which proved an early foray for the young boy into a forbidden adult world of sex, violence, and glamor at once familiar and exotic. His recollection of playing with a toy 007 briefcase— whose fake gun he supplemented with his own passport and military ID— betray the rapidly deteriorating inner life of a child incapable of coping with the pressures of the adult world foisted onto him from too early an age.

It was an inner life that went from crumbling to annihilated when the elder Landis was transferred yet again, this time to New Orleans. Here, the circumstances of Bill's life become even murkier; he spoke about this period rarely and only in ellipticals, using the bluntest yet vaguest of language. "I had my first blackout experience, which was not induced by any drug. I was raped—I never knew by whom... no one in my family would acknowledge it. That day ended my childhood. I was a six-year-old man, and in the military men are taught to tolerate the pain—to take it like a man." Those few words— almost an aside in "Body for Rent"—

encapsulate the entirety of his adolescence, and yet speak volumes about the man they would produce and the damage that he would carry with him for the rest of his life. It was an epochal event that would set the pattern both for Bill's life trajectory and the way he would interact with other human beings. The perpetrator(s) were never caught. Bill's father quietly retired from the Air Force, and with no recognition of the trauma the boy had survived, the Landises moved to New York City circa the mid-1960s to be near his maternal grandparents.

The New York of this age, on the cusp of 1950s *I Love Lucy* sophistication and *Taxi Driver* urban hellscape— "The *Midnight Cowboy* era" as Bill himself would phrase it— proved to be a fertile environment for fostering the imagination of a traumatized, naturally inquisitive and preternaturally intelligent child (by the time he reached high school, he'd already been skipped ahead two years due to his academic abilities, making him a very young freshman at thirteen). The constant moves, sense of placelessness, and lack of cultural identity (Bill was of mixed French and Greek ancestry and, due to his dark complexion, would later pass for Hispanic amongst New York's Puerto Rican population) had a major impact on him; as he would later tell writer Clayton Patterson, "I have always identified with surrealists like Alejandro Jodorwosky and Fernando Arrabal of the Panic Theater - you're born in one nation, spend your childhood in another country, then move to yet another one, with your ethnicity having nothing to do with any of it. So no place is home; you get a sense of permanent displacement. A feeling that contributes a quality of unreality."

Initially living in Brooklyn, the Landises soon found themselves on Staten Island. Here, Bill would accompany his grandfather to a Greek men's social club, slipping away to sneak into the adult movie theater next door, where he struggled to reconcile his own burgeoning sexuality with his assault in Louisiana. It was around this same time that the young Bill would see his first film by notorious exploitation director Andy Milligan (*Guttertrash,* as he remembers it), and, together with his adult theater forays, the twin cinematic experiences proved formative. Indeed, the specters of sex and violence— sometimes separate, sometimes intertwined— loomed large over Landis' formative years. Growing volatile in retirement, his father began lashing out at the men around him, including Bill's grandfather, who was eventually placed into a nursing home for his own protection. His subsequent death there-- elderly and isolated from his loved ones-- had a profound impact on the young Bill, who "resolved to do everything in my power not to age... film seemed like a medium that could preserve my youth forever."

Concurrently, Bill developed an emotionally and sexually complex relationship with another girl his age who lived in the same apartment building and who shared his growing fascination with the intersection between the erotic and the violent. Perhaps as a natural inclination, perhaps in an attempt to reframe and gain control over his own experiences, Landis developed an early fascination for S&M— particularly the submissive role— that would not only define his adolescence but go on to impact the perspective of his later film criticism and the trajectory of his young life. "It was overwhelming, sexually exciting, and involved physical pain, which made me a bit afraid," Landis would recall of his young girlfriend, whom he gave the pseudonym Kelly in "Body for Rent." "The vague notion of death was in there, but I didn't know quite how." The pair's relationship was characterized by childish games that escalated in intensity and adult undertones, from her encouraging him to spy on her through his peephole while she played in the hallway to his holding her ankles while she dumpster dived, to, ultimately, her ritualistically whipping him with her jump rope in what proved for Bill to be his second foundational sexual experience, further establishing for him a link between emotional and physical pain and pleasure, acceptance, and love. "I had an involuntary orgasm; I just couldn't help it. When she got rough I associated it with affection and excitement."

Unfortunately, Bill's relationship with Kelly proved short lived. By virtue of his being skipped ahead, Landis found himself forced to associate with boys and girls older, more mature, and more worldly than himself, resulting in a loss of the normal rites of passage that define an adolescence and further instilling in him a sense of loss, isolation, and otherness. Watching Kelly going to school in her uniform, to experience a normal childhood with all its social opportunities, was another traumatizing incident in a steadily increasing chain. By the time he was sixteen, Landis had already graduated high school— where he'd found some solace as the paper's film critic (a teacher wrote him a note encouraging him to "expand beyond reviews," as he recalled to Bruun). He was soon enrolled in the NYU Stern School of Business, further alienating him from his peers and thrusting him into the quasi-adult world of campus politics and social mores, barely old enough to drive, five years too young to drink.

In a desperate effort to achieve some sense of normalcy he began dating a classmate whom he remembered as a "well meaning but neurotic girl;" however, the courtship proved to be disastrous. Though, by his own recollection, she attempted to give Bill something approximating a normal teenage dating experience, he found himself crippled by her sexual overtures, unable to bring himself to undress in front of her in spite of his own eagerness— the classic sexual abuse survivor's paradox of wishing to at once reclaim and simultaneously deny one's own sexuality. Bill discovered himself, instead, finding mental— if not physical— solace in the presence of his girlfriend's immediate family: "What I enjoyed about visiting my girlfriend was when I'd be the only man in the house, the center of attention for her, her younger sister, and her youngish divorcee mother... I wanted them to gang up and get as rough as they wanted on me." Ultimately, the relationship couldn't sustain, and the pair broke up. The failure of one of his first attempts at a normal, healthy, adolescent experience presaged his descent into obsessively watching hardcore pornography at adult theaters and reading S&M literature, a foray that culminated in his contacting a prostitute via an ad in *Screw* magazine and having his first consensual sexual experience, on his own terms: "I didn't want to be with a nervous teen. I never liked the thought of a girl collecting my cherry, so I collected it myself."

Though the experience apparently offered Bill some catharsis, like so many assault survivors, he still found himself with a sense of helplessness and lack of control. His first encounter with consensual sex had left him hungry for more. Combined with the volatility of being pressured into business school by his parents and the mounting sense of a lost childhood, it proved a vicious combination, especially for an angry young man in an era that encouraged anonymous sex as a badge of masculinity and lacked a vocabulary for treating male sexual abuse survivors. In Bill's own words, "I got angry. I stopped going to school; I just read the books and passed the tests... I had just turned 18. There were all sorts of freaky scenes to explore. Clubs for every persuasion. I participated in gang bangs, pissed on strangers lying in troughs, fisted masochists in front of enthralled voyeurs. I punched, kicked, and shoved. There was never a shortage of willing victims, although more of them were male than female. Manhattan was a floating Roman orgy, but it was a cold and anonymous party."

Assessing his later perspective on gender roles in the media and his deconstruction of modes of masculinity and machismo in film— indeed, one could argue that Bill was both unironically embodying and exposing toxic masculinity in his writing decades before that became an acknowledged concept— it's fascinating to note that it was around this period he began exploring his own bisexuality. Equally fascinating is that it's a word he never used to self-describe: while his writings are filled with erotic assessments of the male form and praise for the physical beauty and sexuality of male actors and porn stars, and he himself would document his own sexual encounters with men and women, 'bisexual' appears, literally, to have been a word not in his vocabulary. Like many men of his generation, Landis seemed reticent to acknowledge the psycho-sexual realities of being attracted to both men and women, even if he readily discussed the mechanical practicalities of it. Whatever the case, his emotional drive always seemed to have been towards achieving the sexual approval of women, as he recalled: "I tried to give myself confidence; I seemed to need a lot of it. My one consistent admirer was one of my mother's friends, a schoolteacher who would slip me $50 bills when I'd tell her salacious stories about New York's wild side. She never demanded any sex. I never offered. But I did get the *Midnight Cowboy* delusion of getting kept by an older woman."

In 1980, Bill Landis was arguably— at least on the surface— among the most privileged young men of immediate pre-Reagan New York City. He already had a master's degree and would, in short order, find himself employed by Merril Lynch and Con Edison (to hear Bill tell it at least; no two sources consulted for this book were able to identify him as working the same job at the same place at the same time). There, his knowledge of business and technology proved invaluable as one of the first generation of men to integrate the computer into the 9-5 workday. Now living on his own in Manhattan, free from the yoke of his parents' expectations, Landis found himself in a situation imminently familiar to many who spend their formative years enduring trauma, struggling to survive it, and finding themselves controlled by more powerful forces: Now that he was finally free, he was paradoxically more at a loss than ever before to make his own destiny. "I just couldn't deal with the prison of an office," Landis would later write. "The hourglass of my life was always in my face. Apart from that vague childhood ambition of becoming a movie star, an international sex symbol like Ursula Andress, I didn't know what to do with my life."

At the age of twenty-one, Bill Landis was finally absolutely free— and absolutely trapped.

2. MR. SLEAZOID

History needs to be recorded in all its human, cultural and psychological forms, with all three overlapping. And I've never written fiction because truth was always far more surreal.

Bill Landis

At a key moment in his seminal work *Fear and Loathing in Las Vegas,* Hunter S. Thompson— whose style and journalistic purpose was often compared with Bill's—wrote, "It seems like a lifetime, or at least a Main Era—the kind of peak that never comes again. San Francisco in the middle sixties was a very special time and place to be a part of." Those very words could just as easily apply to Manhattan's 42nd Street as it existed at the dawn of the 1980s. It was paradoxically both at the height of its cultural power and entering the great nadir of its ultimate decline, before Koch and Giuliani and crack and AIDS all coalesced to bring an end to an entire subculture and way of life that Bill would desperately scramble to document and preserve before it vanished from the face of the earth forever. The cataclysmic 1977 New York riots—which had left the Deuce curiously untouched—were three years in the past. The strip of 42nd Street between 7th and 8th avenue that served as home to what seemed like innumerable movie theaters, sex shops, arcades, junk stores, and whatever else the vice scene needed to thrive had seemingly entered a new golden age. It was a time when the dazzling innovation of video tape promised to revitalize the street in a way it had never seen before. Suddenly, adult entertainment was available for home consumption (albeit at significant cost), away from the prying eyes—and avaricious switchblades—of the seediest Times Square theaters. If you could afford the VCR and high-priced tapes, though, the thrill of seeing strangers fuck on film was suddenly right there at your fingertips, with rewind, slo-mo, and pause features to boot.

What was more, the advent of in-theater video projectors meant a sort of grindhouse renaissance; in previous eras, the Deuce had served as a very unique sort of cinematic ecosystem. Exploitation movies—often locally produced ones, like the work of Andy Milligan, Roger Watkins, and Mike and Roberta Findlay—premiered on Forty-Deuce, showed for a week (if that), and, if they weren't raking in the big bucks, quickly faded into obscurity, never to be seen by Manhattanite eyes again unless some generous (or desperate) theater owner decided to revive them on a double or triple feature alongside something more marketable.

Video, though, meant the return of the repressed, with cinematic obscurities of yesteryear sharing marquee space with today's greatest hits. It was imminently conceivable that a patron could pay $5 for a ticket and watch *Love Me Deadly* alongside *Flashdance*, the Mr. Rogers-sploitation slasher *The Psychopath* back-to-back with the latest *Friday the 13th*. On the streets, the Deuce was dying—hustling, as a way of life, had brought "gay cancer"—soon to be codified in medical texts and later the mainstream press as AIDS—to Times Square with a vengeance, and before the end of the decade, a significant number of the city's vice workers had succumbed to its cruelty. Those who dodged that bullet were often taken out by a variety of drug addictions, nominally crack cocaine. In the theaters, though, a whole new world had emerged. Far away from the corporate, studio-dominated movie theaters of middle-America, the Deuce provided filmgoers with the opportunity to see underground, independent, grass-roots, foreign-produced films that would never show in any AMC or Cinemark. It was an age of rediscovery; it was an era of innovation; it was the dawn of *Sleazoid Express*.

Bill Landis had been a writer from a young age, penning his first film review when he was eleven; later, at age fourteen, he read Hubert Selby's *Last Exit to Brooklyn*, a transformative experience that demonstrated to him the subversive power of prose. "It opened my eyes in many ways," he would later tell Carl Abrahamsson.

"One was that you could write about anything, no matter how shocking, so long as it was humanly true." It was an ethos Landis would learn to apply as he entered his twenties.

Newly graduated from NYU with a master's degree in finance, he was drifting in a sort of netherworld between arrested adolescence and forced adulthood, dissatisfied with life and looking for something more. Wall Street paid his bills but didn't fulfill his soul. Landis could put on a coat and tie and do the nine-to-five grind, but come quitting time, he bounced straight to 42nd Street for what seemed like the beginning of his *real* life—still in the coat-and-tie, mind you. One of the defining aesthetic features of Landis' early years as a grindhouse scholar was his commitment to the trappings of midcentury sartorial edicts, which both made him at home amongst the Deuce's squarejohn collection of Mad-Ave thrill seekers and a standout from its t-shirt and jeans homebrew film crowd.

He was hardly new to the scene—Landis had first glimpsed 42nd upon his family's move to NYC, and developed an early curiosity about it during his parents' many forays to more respectable Broadway Shows. He'd dipped his toes in more deeply as a teen, telling Patterson, "I had been hanging around 42nd Street since I was 16, using a fake ID card in the early 1970s, then shortly after going to the LES to concerts at CBGS and a lot of the fly by night after hours clubs." As a bored NYU student, he'd begun skipping classes to hit double-and-triple features with friend and classmate John LeMoss, often seeing up to nine films a week, per a late-in-life interview with journalist Carl Abrahamsson. He was also a regular at New York's storied Club 57, an ersatz art café that earned its "underground" status literally, being hosted in the basement of a Polish Catholic church that turned a blind eye to the freaky scene unfolding on its premises. It was there that Landis met and befriended future *Psychotronic* founder and editor-in-chief, Michael J. Weldon, with whom he bonded over their shared love of exploitation cinema. Weldon would later give a nod to Bill in the first issue of his own zine, which debuted a few months after *Sleazoid Express.*

"I met him before he started his paper," Weldon recalls. "There was another guy involved in *Psychotronic* from the very beginning named Charlie Beesley. I met Bill either through Charlie or by going to 57 with Charlie. Charlie and I actually helped Bill move from his parents' place on Staten Island. He lived in quite a few places before he got the apartment on 14th. He lived with a really good underground filmmaker who was doing some videos at the time. He lived on 9th street, and that didn't work out for very long, and then he lived in a hotel—a tiny room in a hotel for a while—and a bit later he got the place on 14th street. When I first met him he was really into Herschell Gordon Lewis movies. He had a projector, and he owned prints of some of them. He screened some of those at Club 57, and he screened them and some other movies at the Mud Club."

While Lewis' oeuvre may have been Bill's passion at the dawn of the 80s, it was one film in particular that sparked his imagination and spurred him to take his adolescent writing to another level: Doris Wishman's 1978 mockumentary *Let me Die a Woman,* an early trans-rights film incorporating intimate, unflinching interviews with transgender individuals and sex confirmation doctors with lurid reenactments of their personal experiences. Fascinated by the film and its subject matter and convinced that no one would ever seriously review it, Bill typed up a review (in a room at the George Washington hotel), copied it, and began disseminating it wherever he could, handing out copies to strangers at his regular haunts throughout Manhattan.

What began as a whim soon turned into a vocation. Landis had offered the New York underground something it had never seen before: a serious—albeit perfunctory—critical analysis of a non-mainstream film that addressed a subject matter considered verboten by polite society. The response was positive; it's easy to imagine the impact it must have had on Bill, who'd gone from overbearing home life to overwhelming academic experience to overstimulated adult real-world before he was legally old enough to drink. Soon, Bill found himself not only a member but a fixture of the burgeoning 1980s New York underground art scene, the same milieu that would be immortalized in fiction by Tama Janowitz in her *Slaves of New York* stories. His ticket to acceptance: *Sleazoid Express,* which rolled off the presses in 1980 as a one-sheet, biweekly newsletter containing brief, telegraph-style, stream-of-consciousness critiques, analyses, and reviews of the films too salacious, obscure, and obscene for mainstream publications. At the heart of the publication was a you-are-there ethos, as Bill would often return to his recently acquired 14th-street between 2nd-and-3rd avenue apartment (the same block where Travis Bickle lives in *Taxi Driver*) immediately after leaving a film and write it up in an off-the-cuff frenzy. The specifics of the movie weren't always correct; details would sometimes be fudged, but there was an authenticity to his writing that justified any minor narrative misremembrances. "He was one of the best writers I've ever read, but, not always consistent with the facts," recalls a friend who wishes to remain anonymous. "It was hard to tell what was truth, what was reality, and what was in his brain. He had a lot of chemical issues."

Prior to Landis, horror and exploitation film journalism had been relegated to the Forest J. Ackerman crowd, loving odes to Universal Horror and Hammer Pictures (the latter studio's output would prove a thorn in Landis' side when one of their productions popped up on a Deuce triple-feature—not raw enough, he felt; too restrained). Rarely were genre films looked at from a critical or deeper analytical perspective. *Fangoria*, which first broke the mold of fan-tribute zines, had just debuted the year before *Sleazoid*, but was still nominally concerned with being a fusion sci-fi, horror, and fantasy magazine dedicated to behind-the-scenes photos and SFX tutorials. It had only run its first exclusively-horror themed installment— the famous "*Shining* issue," Vol. 1, #7—a few months before *Sleazoid* hit the streets, and even then it still shied away from covering independent horror cinema in favor of studio fare. *Sleazoid* went where politer publications dared not tread. If *Fangoria* had a certain heavy metal ethos, *Sleazoid* was punk through-and-through, down to its DIY aesthetic and irregular publication schedule (though it ostensibly moved from a bi-weekly to monthly format, numerous issues contain disclaimers from Bill apologizing for delays or explaining that special double-issues were meant to compensate for missing earlier editions).

As he published *Sleazoid,* Bill found himself becoming more of a recognizable figure in the early-80s underground scene, befriending Warhol superstar Ondine, with whom he shared a brief but fruitful relationship in stage production. In between sojourns to Indian restaurants around Manhattan (exploring international cuisine being a favorite pastime, as friend Art Ettinger would later recall), the pair staged an off-off-Broadway production of Landis' own stage play *The Life of Raymond Burr,* a satire purporting to document the (imaginary) sexual proclivities of the eponymous TV legend, featuring Ondine as the desk chair-confined lead. The show premiered at Club 57. While 42nd may have been Bill's spiritual home and 14th his literal one, in the early years of his reign as the King of the Sleaze Scene, Club 57 was something approximating his headquarters, selling copies of *Sleazoid,* debuting Landis' own shows (one notorious performance art piece found Bill, playing Jim Jones, reciting the cult leader's infamous final speech while leading the audience in drinking Kool Aid), and serving as the venue for his burgeoning career as a film distributor. As much as he may have loved (and excelled at) writing about movies, his dreams lay in exhibition—he wanted to be the man responsible for reviving lost classics and discovering new ones, and Club 57 was the prime place to begin diving deeper into those waters. It was the perfect venue to meet and interact with other artistic minds; it was through his time at 57 that Bill made the acquaintance of underground filmmakers such as Beth and Scott B, in whose film *Vortex* he appeared in a brief role as "Patient."

Club 57 would also prove to be the locale where Bill formed one of his most significant friendships. Jimmy McDonough had moved back home to New York at the age of 20 after a childhood spent split between Chicago, New Jersey, and Louisiana—an upbringing that was equal parts "*Happy Days* and *Hee Haw*" as he would later recall to John Szpunar in his indispensable tome *Xerox Ferox*. As intrinsically drawn to 42nd Street as Bill, McDonough became one of *Sleazoid*'s earliest readers, ultimately finding himself at 57 one evening to catch a performance of *Burr* to see what Bill was all about. The night would prove cataclysmic, as Ondine came onstage under the influence of drugs, and, partway through the performance, broke character and began to criticize the quality of Bill's writing. When it was all said and done, McDonough approached Bill with some consoling words; the pair struck up a friendship, and, before long, he found himself contributing to *Sleazoid*. The relationship proved fruitful, if not in the ways one might expect.

"The material I wrote on my own was often the worst crap in the magazine," McDonough told Szpunar. "I literally didn't know how to form a sentence... but Bill gave me a chance." At the same time, McDonough's advice and guidance proved invaluable— he was the one who encouraged Bill to lean deeper into his "you-are-there" reportage and allow more of his personal interests to shine through in the publication. This led Bill to shy away from strict film criticism and delve deeper into the ethnographic and intimate aspects of *Sleazoid* that would continue to set it apart from other publications and become its defining feature. While other magazines of the day may have had "letters to the editor" pages, *Sleazoid* had a much more personal "Letters to Bill"—or "Mr. Sleazoid," as he had taken to calling himself—page; respondents were often teenagers and young adults (probably invented ones, according to Weldon—"Bill and Jimmy made up all kinds of stuff, including names and fake letters") to whom Bill gave personalized and sincere, if not misguided, advice on topics ranging from body image to proper drug use.

While some (or most) of the correspondents may have been fake, one was very much real: future *Deep Red* scribe Greg Goodsell, who began a years-long pen-and-paper relationship with Bill after writing to *Sleazoid,* allowing him a glimpse behind the curtain of the burgeoning zine culture Bill had helped jumpstart. "I would always send him an encouraging letter after each issue, and he'd always reply very quickly," Goodsell told me. "He was very good about written correspondence."

Another of Bill's correspondents was Pennsylvania projectionist and local Deuce celebrity "Mad" Ron Roccia, who lent his name (and collection of 35mm trailers—the largest in America at the time) to *Mad Ron's Prevues from Hell*, a VHS trailer compilation that would serve as a generation of suburban kids' gateway drug into exploitation cinema at the end of the 80s. "I had gotten in touch with him through the mail," Roccia recalls of finding an ad Bill had put out. "He was advertising *Sleazoid Express* and selling issues of a magazine called *Violent World*. I bought every issue of *Violent World* that he had and started subscribing to *Sleazoid*, and we started corresponding a bit. We had a couple of disputes about movies that he loved and I didn't, and vice versa. We argued heavily [but] he was friendly. He was very opinionated, and definitely stuck by his guns. If he didn't care for something, he didn't care for it. There was no convincing him of something's quality if he didn't think it had it. He hated Bill Lustig's *Maniac*, and *Maniac* was one of my favorites of all time. And he hated it. He couldn't get past it. And I was like, 'Come on, Bill, this is exactly what you've been looking for. What the Hell are you thinking?' And he hated *Creepshow* for being 'corporate.' I was like, 'C'mon, Bill, it's George Romero. How corporate is George?' He had some very odd opinions." Over the course of their relationship, Roccia advocated watching moves on the Deuce under the influence of LSD, an idea that intrigued Bill: "It makes everything much more intense," Roccia recalls of his advice to Bill. "Instead of watching it, you're living it; and if you're jaded by horror, you're *not* jaded anymore. All of a sudden, you need to *survive* the thing. It's become *personal*." Bill took the suggestion to heart and began dosing himself with acid prior to screenings; as he would later recount, as a result of his LSD consumption, he began to discover hidden "meanings" in the films he was watching, beginning a new phase of his critical career.

With McDonough's encouragement, Bill—like Hunter S. Thompson before him— didn't just critique films, though: he recreated and preserved an *experience*. Readers were just as likely to hear Bill's opinion on *Videodrome* as they were to encounter his blow-by-blow documentation of a fistfight that had occurred in the lobby before the show or be regaled by tales of hustlers working the mens' room of a given theater. *Sleazoid* wasn't just about exploitation films: it was about the people who watched and made them, and the environment that preserved them. It was the trade publication of Times Square, if not the Grindhouse Theater Scene, before the word grindhouse had been made household lingo by Tarantino and Rodriguez. In time, a third, eminently mysterious figure would join the Sleazoid triumvirate— "Buggin' Out," who—per McDonough-- briefly roomed with Bill and who contributed several iconic collage covers for the zine. As of 2021, his identity remains a mystery-- if he even existed. Most individuals queried for this book—including Michael Weldon—believe him to have been a fictional character created by Bill and

McDonough, although McDonough maintains he was real. Nonetheless, McDonough declined to identify him to Szpunar for Ferox and similarly plead the fifth to my own inquiries. Like Landis, Buggin' Out remains a figure who exists on the periphery of reality, only a few vague clues to his identity available ("a musician and... a cook" McDonough told Szpuar, further elaborating that, somewhere, there exists a tape of Buggin' Out and Landis in an impromptu jam session, with Bill on vocals, serving as proof of his existence). Despite McDonough's insistence, though, a friend of Bill's who wishes to remain anonymous cited a letter dated circa 2005 in which Landis calls Buggin' Out "just a deflection from a first-person viewpoint," while Kurt Loder, when queried for memories of the *Rolling Stone* profile he wrote on Bill (which contains mention of Buggin' Out), claimed that he was simply a character played by McDonough.

With McDonough on board, the publication entered a sort of golden era. McDonough provided the structure, Bill the raw material. The two would watch films and prowl forty-deuce together, talking things out, allowing Bill to return home later to commit thoughts to the page. "A lot of stuff came out of what I call routines," McDonough told Szpunar. "Stuff we'd talk about while walking to this theater or that. We came up with a whole lingo that went along with it... We'd talk these things into the ground." That lingo became one of *Sleazoid*'s—and Bill's—defining features, with Landis developing a unique patois, linguistic tics, and shibboleths that gave the zine a distinct flavor and sense of place. Issues were littered with references to such individuals as "popeyes" ("men created by pornography" Bill would explain to Kurt Loder in the career-making *Rolling Stone* profile—or, more elaborately, working-class men, often with a background in dock work or manual labor, characterized as much by their closely-shorn hair and work clothes as their desperate need to consume hardcore films round the clock), and "blockheads" (excessively-muscled bodybuilders, often in denial about their own sexuality), among innumerable other ethnographic descriptors Bill assigned to the various types he saw wandering 42nd every day.

Too, *Sleazoid* became confrontational and topically complex in a way that other contemporary genre magazines didn't dare. While *Famous Monsters* was all fawning reminiscence about the Golden Age of horror and *Fangoria* functioned as something of a precursor to the internet in bringing readers behind-the-scenes information on upcoming films, *Sleazoid* sought to challenge readers' expectations about film and film criticism, deconstruct genre convention, and, most of all, turn an analytical eye on society itself. One need look no further than the infamous "Led Zeppelin Issue," published in the Spring of 1983, which itself serves as an encapsulation of the whole *Sleazoid* ethos. "INSIDE! LED ZEPPELIN—FAGGOTS?" blares the headline to the issue's primary story, stamped in bold at the bottom of the cover page. The uninitiated could be forgiven for expecting the story to be an AIDS-era homophobic diatribe against Zeppelin's gender-bending aesthetic;

rather, the antagonistic title serves to pull readers into a story that takes a double-pronged attack. While the article's apparent purpose is to review the seminal Zeppelin rock documentary *The Song Remains the Same,* it also turns into a thought-provoking essay on gender identity, with Landis assessing the performative aspects of gender and low-key codifying concepts that today we would recognize as gender fluidity and non-binary identification. In the same issue, Landis tackles misogyny in genre film ("This movie has a hostile edge, that of a penis worshipper who dislikes women" he writes of *Screwballs,* which he admits he liked despite writing it up under the title "*Scumballs*") before presenting the reader with ironic cheesecake centerfold photos of himself in a variety of homoerotic tableaux, complete with awkwardly placed Converse sneakers.

Decades before the explicit intersection of genre writing, sociology, and concepts of social justice, *Sleazoid Express* was already tackling these ideas, albeit in an intentionally provocative, irreverent, and iconoclastic way. Notably, Landis never assumed that white heterosexuality was the default in describing either cinematic characters or denizens of 42nd Street, although some of the coarser language employed to describe gender-nonconforming individuals or members of particular groups wouldn't fly in 2021. The tone was never one of targeted malice, though; Bill cast an askew glance on humanity in general. It was a look at exploitation and horror cinema that fans weren't used to reading, oftentimes about films they'd never heard of.

Often, they were films people never *would* have heard of if it weren't for *Sleazoid*.

"To call him a trailblazer is an understatement," says Art Ettinger, editor of *Ultra Violent* magazine, who was not only inspired by *Sleazoid* but who formed a close relationship with Bill later in life. "*Sleazoid Express* was one of the only publications that, at the time, was covering 42nd Street in the way that he did."

"Bill really brought the joy of discovery," Goodsell says. "He saw a very obscure movie and it had qualities that everybody else disregarded. He could laugh along with the film if it was cheesy and inept. Sometimes it's more entertaining than a serious film that succeeds... He pulled Andy Milligan out of the gutter and gave his films an appreciation that wasn't there previously. It was all dismissed as junk. But the movies of Andy Milligan were very bad artistry, and they were deeply personal, and Bill communicated the joy that low-budget schlock movies brought—that they were put out by people who had nothing to lose and they just put their vision out there and had no apology about it."

"Bill was covering movies that *nobody* else covered, *and* talking about The Deuce. That was my playground and someone, *exclusively*, was covering my playground!" Roccia says of the excitement 42nd street denizens felt at seeing themselves represented seriously in print.

"He was a lively example of someone who takes an intense interest in a despised cultural backwater and treats it as a subject for serious inquiry," says Kurt Loder.

"In this regard, I think his enthusiasm for Z movies mirrored similar attitudes among fans of punk and garage rock – these were new pop subcultures. Unlike *Psychotronic,* I don't think *Sleazoid* could ever have built even a semi-mainstream audience— it was more hardcore and unflinching than Michael Weldon's mag, which was amiable and almost jaunty by comparison— fun, in other words. Bill, on the other hand, could talk knowledgeably about denizens of the porn scene and other precincts of the cinematic abyss. I don't think he had the common touch… I think it must be hard to imagine, today, in our trivia-clogged culture, what a kick all of this stuff seemed to be at the time. Suddenly there was a whole boatload of new pop ephemera to obsess about. If these two mags didn't create a new movie audience— the fans were already there, waiting— they certainly helped identify it."

"The thing that's worth remembering is back then, there was no internet," says *Trashola* founder Jim Morton. "What Bill and, to a lesser extent, myself and Michael Weldon and Tim Lucas and everybody else were doing was— we just had to find this stuff in a library, you know? We had to just dig through stuff in the library and go through old newspapers and find books… It was very hard to do back then. I remember back then, none of us could find Herschel Gordon Lewis, he had just disappeared off the face of the map… The one thing that is being lost, and I think Bill has contributed an important canon of work to, is the movie theater experience."

"I looked at Bill as being more of a scholar," recalls Keith Crocker, who found *Sleazoid* to be a thoughtful counterpoint to Rick Sullivan's more acerbic *Gore Gazette*, and who ultimately bonded with Bill over his own zine, *The Exploitation Journal*. "He tended to take himself seriously. There was humor, there was definitely humor in his writing but it was subtle… With Bill, it was something that, as you were reading along, you got the idea that he was riffing on something. But I always took him as being a little more intellectual and reading into cinema. He really read into cinema, which fascinated me. He gave the independent low budget film more reason to exist than, say, to put money into the pockets of some producer who was jumping on some kind of trend. Bill could actually see meaning and worth in these films and how they paralleled the times."

While the zine flourished and his collaboration with McDonough proved successful, not all of Landis' partnerships from this era in his life would prove positive. Most notably, in 1982, Bill had the opportunity to contribute to *Fangoria*, penning a considerable article on/interview with Andy Milligan that ran in Vol. 1, #20—something made possible with the help of "Mad" Ron, after their first—and only—in-person meeting.

"It was a very interesting meeting," Roccia says. "I'm sorry it was only once. It was at the 8th Street Playhouse. And I told him where to find Andy Milligan." As luck would have it, Roccia had been contemplating starting his own VHS distribution label to take advantage of the burgeoning home video market, and had contacted Milligan's business partner to inquire about potentially acquiring his films: "I sat and watched *Legacy of Blood* with Andy's business partner at The Lyric. At the time I was half-full of myself, thinking that I could release all the Andy Milligan films on videotape. We had this whole long talk and he says 'Come on, I'm gonna take you to meet Andy.' I don't remember the partner's name, but he brought me just three blocks away, to where Andy was directing two plays in the same building at the same time! He had an upstairs play and a downstairs play, and he was directing both of them! He was really friendly. Loved putting his arm around me. Wonderful conversation. It must have been within a week or two that the *Blood Feast* screening came around and I said to Bill, 'You know, Andy Milligan has a play going on.' He was like, 'Really?' I told him all about Andy, and the next thing you know Bill's got that big Andy Milligan interview in *Fangoria*!"

The *Fangoria* interview was a success, the beginning of what could—and should—have been a groundbreaking professional relationship, representing one of the few times that underground exploitation cinema was represented in the magazine during its initial run. Any hopes of Bill using the publication to bring 42nd Street into the mainstream were quickly squashed, though, when his follow-up pitch proved to be too controversial for *Fangoria*'s Bob Martin. For his next act—as a means of bringing queer cinema into the mainstream— Bill wanted to begin reviewing pornographic films in the pages of the magazine, beginning with the loops of underground gay filmmaker Toby Ross. At the time, many gay filmmakers were relegated to making adult films if they wished to artistically express themselves, and Bill saw in Ross' movies not cheap exploitation but legitimate artistic merit, and he wanted the opportunity to both help legitimize queer cinema and introduce readers of *Fangoria* to a new world. "That was brave on the part of Bill because there was a lot of homophobia directed at the gay community," Goodsell recalls. "Martin was scandalized to the point that he effectively blacklisted Bill from ever writing for *Fangoria* again." (Bob Martin passed away in 2020 during the writing of this book, before he could respond to a request for comment).

"I got a snippet of Bob Martin's correspondence," Goodsell says. "Martin wrote to *Film Comment* and said that Bill was promoting child pornography." (Ross specialized in films featuring "twinks," young homosexual men in their late teens to early 20s with a youthful, boyish appearance). "Bob Martin actively persecuted Bill and went to people who were accepting his freelance writing, saying that he's a terrible person who promotes child pornography… [Bill] probably lost a few of his readers on account of that, but he was very brave."

Years later, assessing the response to his Toby Ross work, Landis would wryly remark to Carl Abrahamsson: "Anything that's sexually ambiguous makes these nerds very nervous."

The incident not only caused Bill to double-down

on making *Sleazoid* a success, but led to an ongoing war with *Fangoria* and Martin, who never offered a formal apology. For the duration of Sleazoid's run, "*Fangoria*" was used as a byword to describe any film he found lacking in artistic merit but excessive in blood and gore, and he occasionally took potshots at the magazine by suggesting that they should be covering a given film instead of him (the aforementioned Zeppelin issue even features one such "shoutout" regarding *Don't Go in the Woods,* further establishing its credentials as *the* consummate *Sleazoid*).

The rancor was hardly reserved for *Fangoria,* though. Bill came to see other zines not as further contributions to the field of grindhouse journalism but personalized attacks against him meant to steal his glory. "Bill was angry," Crocker says. "He felt that people were riding on what he did, but that was not the truth." Jim Morton concurs: "He had a certain amount of contempt for Rick Sullivan because, according to Bill, the first issue of *Gore Gazette* was essentially a tackle on Bill… Rick Sullivan was probably not saying bad things about Bill, but he had one or two sentences—knowing what I know about Rick Sullivan, it was probably something along the lines of, 'He spent too much time talking about sexploitation and not about horror movies' or something like that."

Gary Hertz, a writer for *Gore Gazette* who would later go on to have a career with New Line Cinema, feels that Sullivan may have encouraged Bill's ire: "Bill was—I don't want to say antisocial, but he was not an outgoing guy. Rick liked to antagonize people, and if there was a rivalry I think it was a rivalry Rick encouraged."

Michael Weldon, too, feels that there was a mutual animosity between the pair: "Bill and Rick had a few similarities and they were rivals. They both were doing the same thing, at least for a while, and then they both went off in different directions. I got along with both those guys even though they couldn't stand each other. They both did nice things for me. They introduced me to people, I hung out with them, or they hung out with me, depending on how you want to look at it… you had to be there to realize how those guys were rivals and went out of their way to irritate each other."

Offering his own assessment of Bill—with whom he crossed paths numerous times at Danceteria and other Deuce haunts— Hertz says: "Bill was a bit of an enigma. He wasn't an outgoing guy. I absolutely thought he was a terrific writer, even when his stuff got dark. I realized much later how consistently strong his writing was. Bottom line, Bill was a good writer. But he wasn't the guy who'd say 'let's go get a beer.' Maybe he was with some people, but I personally never got that sense. I didn't find him antisocial, I just never found him outgoing. He was enigmatic and he was not a particularly gregarious guy in my experience."

Bill's wrath wasn't just restricted to writers and their outlets. Landis' enthusiastic writeup of Joel Reed's *Bloodsucking Freaks* (then being exhibited as *The Incredible Torture Show*) led to the two men meeting; they hit it off and, seeing an opportunity to realize his dreams of being an exploitation distributor, Bill—along with LeMoss—formed a company with Reed. The details of the partnership are just as much lost to time (both Bill and Reed are dead now—indeed, it was Reed's death in 2020 that encouraged a number of tight-lipped members of the grindhouse old guard to finally open up about Bill) as they are to mutual hostility.

Near the end of his life, Bill—in something approaching an invective-filled last-hurrah and (largely imaginary) settling of old scores—wrote a forty-page monograph entitled "The Biography of Joel M. Reed, Director of *Bloodsucking Freaks,* or: Games Con Men Play." Written in a style reminiscent of a yellow journalist in a James Elroy novel, the work is peppered with sensationalistic, jazz-age slang from "lavender streaked" (to refer to closeted homosexuals) to the anachronistic and unsettling "Chinaman." "Games" purports to "expose" Bill's dealings with Reed, which he alleged included emotional and psychological manipulation and sexual blackmail, all with the aim of separating aspiring young filmmakers from their money. The work also takes a bizarre non sequitur detour for an extended anecdote about how Bill once allegedly rescued a former classmate—whom he describes as an openly gay, gun-obsessed, drag queen neo-Nazi— from the influence of the burgeoning white power movement in the 1990s; take from *that* what you will.

Reed, for his part, in John Szpunar's *Blood Sucking Freak: The Life and Films of the Incredible Joel M. Reed,* tells an altogether different story, alleging mental and chemical imbalance on Landis' part as the reason for their tumultuous business relationship. All either party could agree upon was that the partnership ended with Landis stealing a considerable sum of money from their corporate bank account—in Reed's telling, a petty act of theft; in Landis', a heroic bit of maneuvering to rightfully take back his investment in a corrupt organization dedicated to manipulating good-natured but naïve young cinematic aspirants. Curiously enough, while neither would have anything positive to say about the other in their later years, "Mad" Ron recalls an idyllic period in Bill and Reed's relationship, as the pair were in attendance at the *Blood Feast* screening together. "I met him and Joel Reed at the same time. They were very friendly together, which was interesting. No animosity at that point."

In the years following their fallout, Landis would continue to seek some form of "vengeance," ultimately enlisting McDonough in an ongoing campaign of psychological terror against Reed, calling him at all hours of the day and night from a variety of phone numbers, in addition to phoning in take-out orders to his apartment from disparate NYC restaurants and sending him what Reed characterized as "Satanic Postcards"— a story familiar to many other individuals who incurred Bill's wrath. Tales of harassing phone calls and those Satanic Postcards abound, though his targets universally regarded him as a pest as opposed to an actual threat, owing to Bill's diminutive stature and fear of face-to-face confrontation. Reed himself recalled an incident in which, after simply raising his fist at Landis, the latter fled in terror.

The Reed debacle—and its attendant campaign of harassment—betrayed an ever-deepening divide between Bill the grindhouse scholar and Mr. Sleazoid—an individual not so much recognizable as a flesh and blood human being but a burlesque culled directly from one of the very films *Sleazoid* would cover. Indeed, a very divergent image of Bill emerges from the reminisces of those who knew him, both during this period and later in life: the gonzo reporter to some, a quiet and reserved individual to others.

"He was creepy and nerdy but still likeable and fun to talk to," Weldon recalls, before noting the rougher edges of Bill's shifting personality: "Bill obviously changed in a big way. He always was an excessive, eccentric guy, but once he got into hard drugs and porn, he was pretty much a different person... He was a complicated guy." Weldon also witnessed Bill's bizarre obsession with crank calling people—including those he admired—a pastime that led to the dissolution of their friendship around this period: "He used to harass people he was a fan of. Like Jack Smith, who was kind of a minor guy in the underground film world… he was this kind, harmless, gay eccentric who lived in an apartment decorated like Arabian Nights. I went with Bill to meet him and then Bill started going on bragging about how he was calling him up on the phone and harassing him all the time. That's the main reason I stopped hanging out with him… He just had this twisted sense of humor.

He would call people on the phone and harass them, drive them nuts, and then he'd call me up and tell me about it. He got off on doing that; he was like [The Jerky Boys]."

To some, though, Bill only showed a positive, outgoing side of himself, as in the case of "Mad" Ron: "He didn't seem at all tormented," Roccia says. "He was just a happy-go-lucky guy at that time. He was a very friendly, generally jovial guy. I was shocked to hear about all the personal trauma he went through. He didn't show it to me."

"I just found him very direct and honest," Morton remembers. "Maybe a little prickly, but all of my friends are prickly so I can't judge that. I trust prickly people more than people who are always nice. I got along fine with Bill and didn't have any problems with him at all."

Greg Goodsell had perspective on both sides of Bill's personality: "He had sort of an existential style, cut-and-dry. He wrote great letters and I kept them all. He was very darkly humorous... He came off as suave and debonair in his written work, but I've heard from other people that he was quite retiring and shy, and sort of awkward in social situations."

Says Keith Crocker: "There are so many conflicting opinions regarding him, and part of that was created *by* him. He wasn't completely innocent in terms of flaring people up. On the other hand, a lot of it became hearsay, a lot of it became a story handed down to someone else, handed down to someone else... It's very difficult because he was sort of, in many ways, an elusive character. And he wasn't always easy to pin down… getting together with him in person or really trying to solidify a friendship was not very easy. He was very guarded. He was very, very guarded… if you want me to give you a word you want to use, that would be the word more than any."

For as diffident as Bill could be, though, he could be equally supportive of other writers.

"Bill was complimentary of my zine," recalls Crocker. "He wanted to promote and push me. He was looking to push smaller guys. He did it for me, he did it for another guy named Hayden Milligan who is since deceased. He was looking for these guys who were out there who were kind of working under the radar, and he was fascinated with us and connected with us… I even ended up in the *Sleazoid* book: 'Go to Cine Fear Video.'"

Morton had a similar experience: "I started writing about movies back in '81… [I] was directly inspired by *Sleazoid Express*. I had read an article by Bill in I think it was in *New York Rocker*. It was called 'From Tack To Gore'… I'd just started to do *Trashola* as a public thing… I later contacted him; he was very helpful. He and I exchanged a lot of information over the years… he turned me onto some good books like *Sinema*."

As the 80s wore on, the line between Bill and Mr. Sleazoid continued to blur. He lost his last corporate job—quit on principle, to hear it from him; fired for using the company xerox to run copies of *Sleazoid*, to hear it from Greg Goodsell. His retreat from polite society and the abandonment of any pretentions towards white-collar legitimacy were both quick and welcome. In short order, Landis found himself working for the Avon theater chain in a variety of jobs ranging from concession worker to projectionist (Landis would later refer to the chain's employees as "The Avon Gang" in "Games Con Men Play," with the possibly drug-induced insinuation that they were a literal crime family in which he wielded *consigliere*-like power). Concurrently, Bill finally decided to pursue one of his most powerful adolescent fantasies: becoming an adult film star. As *Sleazoid Express* entered the zenith of its popularity and influence in 1983, Bill Landis decided to reinvent himself once again. He had succeeded in burying his trauma and pain once by becoming Mr. Sleazoid, grindhouse impresario and king scholar of the cinematic underground. Next, he would attempt to bury it even further by making an ill-advised attempt to finally reclaim and assert his sexuality in perhaps the most destructive way imaginable. Now, he would become Bobby Spector: porn star.

3. BOBBY SPECTOR

Sometimes you have fantasies... they wear out.
Ecco: The Story of a Fake Man on 42nd Street, by Landis/McDonough

The mid-80s were both a high and low water mark for Bill. *Sleazoid* was arguably at the height of its popularity, counting among its (admittedly few) subscribers Larry McMurtry and Roger Ebert. Along with the burgeoning Splatterpunk literary movement, "sleaze cinema" began to receive mainstream recognition and assessment, briefly making Bill a minor celebrity who was profiled in *The LA Times, Film Comment,* and, most importantly, *Rolling Stone,* where he was interviewed in-depth alongside Michael Weldon by future MTV VJ Kurt Loder in a seminal piece on Times Square titled "Night Creatures." Bill and *Sleazoid* had become genuine cult phenomena, and he at last had recognition as a legitimate genre journalist; what's more, he finally got to live a lifelong dream, actually working on an Andy Milligan film by serving as the focus finder on *Carnage*.

At the same time, Bill was quickly approaching the first of many rock-bottoms. Nominally unemployed other than his low-paying gigs for Avon, he was in desperate need of cash not only to facilitate the operation and upkeep of the zine but also to support his growing drug habit—developed, as he would later tell it, as the result of a Joel Reed-related fight that culminated in his being booted from an ER despite suffering numerous cracked ribs. The story may well have an element to truth to it; contradictorily (as with many things involving Bill), he also made mention later in life of his mother stealing painkillers from him as an adolescent (though he neglected to mention what they'd been prescribed for), in addition to early experiments in smoking marijuana, drinking cough syrup, and taking valium (his mother's—revenge, he claimed, for the pain medication *she* stole from him).

While we can only speculate on the mentality of the deceased, and the trend of "psychological autopsies" is discouraged in the psychiatric community, it's hard not to consider that Bill's behavior was a veritable DSM checklist for someone suffering borderline personality disorder, a psychological disturbance usually brought about as a result of severe, untreated childhood trauma, and characterized by extremely black-and-white thinking, a desperate need for love and acceptance, and irrational, often possessive or aggressive behavior that emerges as the result of either trying to win someone's affection or attempting to punish individuals for real or perceived slights. Bill had become just as likely to form a new friendship with someone as he was to viciously rebuff them and begin a campaign of harassment against them, as he had with Reed. "Bill fell out with everyone sooner or later..." McDonough told Szpunar. "Bill had to have an enemy. And the harassment of that enemy became a twenty-four-hour a day obsession."

Though more often diagnosed in women, borderline personality disorder isn't unheard of in men. Due to the tendency for males to express negative emotions such as depression or loneliness through aggressive, confrontational behaviors, male sufferers are often misdiagnosed as psychopaths and denied proper treatment. Not that treatment was very forthcoming in the 1980s—breakthroughs in treating borderlines only occurred more recently in the history of psychiatry. For a period of time, it was almost accepted that a significant number of borderlines would simply burn out and commit suicide—and self-medicate with sex, narcotics, and alcohol in the interim. Although Bill never appears to have struggled with alcohol abuse, he readily took to the first two in an effort to achieve some sense of control over his own life and sexuality, experimenting with cocaine and briefly becoming a Times Square hustler. Ultimately, though, his sexual ambitions were greater than simply living out his adolescent *Midnight Cowboy* fantasies.

"I found an escape from straight society that also seemed to solve my financial problems," Bill later recalled in "Body for Rent." "I'd become a porno star. I was a consenting adult who never considered the consequences. I didn't think I'd live long enough to see any. I thought it meant easy money, basking in my own glory and having tons of sex partners approach me with cash in their hands. I had no patience for talking girls into things, which made me feel like a cad. I didn't want to hurt anyone's feelings."

As it happened, Bill's entryway into the realm of early-80s homegrown porn would be the same Toby Ross whose films Bill had enthusiastically championed to *Fangoria*. "I found Toby in the basement of the Ninth Circle [bar]," Bill recalled. "We bonded over acid and quaaludes, followed by strong candy-store grass. Toby was a great talker, full of weird stories, and we went back to my apartment and rapped for hours about mutual acquaintances and sex-industry gossip… I knew that Toby's endorsement would immediately bring me two flights up on the golden porno pyramid, above Deuce grunt workers like live-sex-show performers and male dancers."

An accommodating Ross took a series of erotic photos to use as publicity stills; shortly thereafter, fate would seemingly intervene on Bill's behalf when, one night, while working a ticket booth, he found himself face-to-face with one of his adult film idols, George Payne. A veteran of the adult film scene with appearances in a wide variety of pornographic films from gay to straight to bisexual, Payne represented to Landis everything he himself wanted to be: "He was a man of a thousand faces, always offering a new angle, a new look, another refracted image. He had the hands of a man of advanced years, and those hands were known for pushing sex partners to the limits of euphoric pleasure or agonizing pain… I was surprised to see that George was my height, five-seven, and had slimmed down from the tiny Atlas look of his early films. I had the eerie feeling I was looking at myself grown older."

Bill showed Payne the Ross photos, and the old-pro was suitably impressed. The pair struck up a friendship, as the itinerant Payne had taken to using the phone booth at the theater as a sort of office, having given the number out as his business line. Ultimately, Landis invited Payne to become his roommate— "the business school I had always wanted to attend." Payne would later be in the audience when Bill's golden opportunity presented itself: a live-sex-show worker Landis called "April" arrived at the theater one evening in a bind—her partner hadn't shown up for their double act. She and Bill had been platonic friends for six months, and she needed someone she could trust. Both feeling sympathy for the woman and seeing an opportunity for his own star to rise, Bill agreed (Landis' further recollections of April in "Body for Rent" betray a deeper well of empathy and human compassion than the more detached, wry sociopolitical writing of *Sleazoid* would indicate. "For a woman on the chaotic Times Square grind, witnessing a steady parade of flashers each day, April had remained surprisingly whole—not at all hard-bitten or cold-blooded, which is the Darwinist road female sex workers who [sic] usually forced to take if they don't want to get killed. But the only empowerment she felt was that she had survived another day.")

Landis went onstage with April and performed with aplomb, even managing to ejaculate on-cue at the end of their allotted fifteen-minute showtime. George Payne watched it all—and he was amazed. He'd seen everything he needed to vouch for Bill as "the new kid." Soon, parts were rolling in; Landis was valued for his youthful appearance, juxtaposed with his larger-than-average endowment ("I was 23, but I looked 13 and my dick seemed bigger than I had ever seen it before") and ability to ejaculate on command. It was this last trait that soon earned him a reputation as one of the best "stunt-cocks" in the New York film scene—men brought in to masturbate to orgasm on-camera in extreme closeups when the male performer in a given scene finds himself unable to climax. He was no longer Bill Landis—he was Bobby Spector, porn god, the name culled from his love of music: "Spector" for legendary producer Phil Spector, "Bobby" because Bill felt that it had a "vaguely doo-wop" feel.

Landis' rise in the porno underworld was meteoric, as he and Payne quickly landed a string of jobs on the kind of porno parodies that are forever being lampooned in other media. Indeed, in a dark counterpoint to Landis' offscreen struggles, his films often had a comic, absurdist bent to them, either from their parodic nature or from Bill's own onscreen presence: gifted with a distinct, nasal, unusually-annunciated Long Island accent an acquaintance once described as "room clearing," he's often silent in his films, (a fact he would later allude to in the final issue of *Sleazoid*), lending some of his performances a bizarre, almost mime-like quality. When he *did* speak onscreen, the results could be equally farcical. The surreal *Parted Lips* concerns the sexual politicking of a court of Slavic aristocrats in exile in 1980s New York, where they're waited on by their servant Ivan Gorkov (Landis), whose Staten Island cadences are a pointed contrast to the faux-Russian accents of some of the other performers, enhancing the film's already unintentional comic ambiance.

Initially, Landis found the experience of being a porn star fulfilling, both financially and emotionally. He was earning one month's rent for two days work, and he settled into a strange but happy routine with George Payne: per "Body for Rent," the pair were starting "each day with a manic jolt, sharing an entire Entenmann's chocolate marshmallow cream cake for breakfast and playing on the telephone like children, pranking enemies in the sex business" before hitting up directors for work. His time in front of the camera gave him the confidence and sense of ownership of his own sexuality that had been taken from him so long ago and which had evaded him ever since; for the first time in his life, it seemed he was at last in control. He gave up hustling, which he'd continued as a monetary sideline/interest, but now pondered a career as a high-paid male escort, hoping to cash in on his celebrity status for big paydays (a short-lived dream that the more pragmatic Payne discouraged). It was also during this period that Landis would later claim he filmed his sole directorial effort, *Rented Eyes,* a supposed cinema verité exploration of 42nd Street vice culture allegedly shot over a 48-hour period. "The startling movie is the only known directorial effort by porn actor Bobby Spector, who shot it on the fly over a weekend and had a brief run but became a regular on the triple bills of the Venus theater located on the 8th avenue strip, even as its cast members and director/star were still working the Times Square circuit," Bill wrote to a friend who wishes to remain anonymous. "It depicts the realities of the situation in Times Square... Cast members utilized in a Warholian manner... Bobby Spector stars as himself... As Bobby leaves work, he runs into his friend Willie, who runs the Satin Ballroom dime-a-dance hooker joint..." Whether the "review" was a tongue-in-cheek joke, a drug delusion, or whether Landis actually filmed something that's now lost to time is anyone's best guess; those closest to Bill in his final years have no knowledge of the film beyond Bill's own writings on it, and those interviewed for this book unanimously agree that it does not exist.

When the cameras weren't rolling, though, Bobby Spector faded from existence, and Bill was stuck with the pain of still being Bill, struggling to accept the truth that a few minutes onscreen couldn't compensate for a lifetime of trauma. "Soon the stress from my sex-kitten career grew too much for my system," he later recalled. He developed anorexia and bulimia, dropping to 105 pounds. Already a recreational cocaine user, he soon began using Percodan after purchasing pills from a theater security guard. "Percodans give a sudden manic surge of euphoria and a sense of sexual excitement, producing an involuntary erection in some men. They also kill mental anguish. Percodans can give you the courage of a lion, but your tolerance rises very quickly and the crash is emotionally devastating," Landis would later write (Bill's use of "Percodans" here betrays a particular linguistic quirk of his, arbitrarily assigning plural designation to singular nouns; he would later discuss "cracks"—not *crack*— in his writing on New York's drug scene). The recreational use soon spiraled into a full-blown dependence, which itself led to his becoming an intravenous drug addict: "My Percodan tolerance was shot to hell; I needed eight pills—$40 worth [about $110 in 2021]—to feel something. So I joined the long line of porn performers who were IV-drug users. The Molotov cocktail of heroin and cocaine, never pharmaceutically consistent when purchased off the streets, made me feel calm, collected, distant, eliminating all my superficial guilt. But the gnawing feeling that I was wasting my life reemerged. Although I thought the speedballs were preserving my youth, they were actually embalming me, and no matter what the medication I'd see the hourglass again. But the rush--the warm feeling from the dope and the excitement of coke-

-was better than any orgasm I had experienced with another human, and I was aware enough to regret it."

Although, in the early days, Bill would perform sober, eventually he was appearing on set already strung out, and his visibly stoned appearance in many of his surviving films lends them a disturbing, estranging quality at odds with their ostensibly erotic tone.

Concurrent to his worsening drug problem, Bill quickly began to see the darker side of the adult film business that lurked beneath the false glamor and sense of sexual empowerment, and any initial feelings of having taken something back soon evaporated into a threatening haze of misogyny, degradation, and dehumanization. "After the sex scenes I'd run to the shower at top speed," he writes "Body for Rent." "If I had done an anal to a woman, I'd vomit immediately. There would be a pileup of women behind me shouting stuff like 'Bobby, please hurry up. I've got three guys' come all over me. It's cold and it's drying… Hurry.' Very empowered." Aggressive directors forced him to beat "willing submissives" who didn't seem quite so willing or submissive; mothers turned out their own reluctant teenage daughters for the promise of fame and a quick buck, bringing their even younger children to set to "acclimate" them to the environment. Writing in the early 90s, Bill even offered an ominous warning about Ron Jeremy, recalling "The constant presence of Ron Jeremy, a fat, obnoxious failed Catskills comedian, was a blight everyone lived with. I've seen girls screaming in pain as he did anals to them… Later, during the editing, moans and music were cut in."

Most damningly for a young man hoping to overcome sexual violence through self-sexual exploitation, the performers were routinely humiliated and objectified, treated as little more than sentient props to be manipulated and cajoled until they'd performed admirably. Bill recalls women so "banged-up" from constant, aggressive sex that they suffered gynecological damage, some to the extent they required corrective surgery. Other male performers, like Bill, turned to drugs to cope with long shooting hours and to give themselves extra stamina, counterintuitively rendering themselves impotent. There is an air of horror around Bill's porn set memories that rivals anything he could've reviewed for *Sleazoid*: "During the sex scenes people would shout orders like drill sergeants. It's a trained dog act--there's nothing 'sex-positive' about it. The women are your coworkers, and you hope that you have some kind of rapport so you can get the job done as easily as possible…The come shot rules your life. It's your existence. You're just fluid in the universe. Your seeds, never to reproduce, are a means to an end."

After a handful of lower-budget successes, Bill finally found his big break when he was cast in a role by director David Darby, a high-caliber pornographer who had produced a string of exploitation and pornographic films going back to the 1970s. While working with Darby should have been a career-making moment for Bill, it only typified everything awful about the industry he'd already come to experience: "Darby bullied me constantly," Landis later recalled in "Body for Rent." "He snatched one of my last joints, smoked it in front of me, pausing as the smoke twirled in front of his swollen slit dark eyes, repeating, 'Bobby, you have to give good acting. But you also have to give good sex.'"

Ironically, the film is one of Bill's silent roles.

"Every time I'd have to do a scene," Bill continued, "he'd stare at my dick and say, 'I wish I was an actor.' Fucking an older woman in the pussy and the ass on a car hood under blaring lights for four hours in the middle of a hot summer night was no easy task. One of the comic-relief episodes had me beat up, but for real, by the guy playing my father. He then threw me out of a second-story window. Also for real. I hated heights anyway, but this was too much. I wanted Darby dead. Still do." During the shoot, Bill was so in fear for his safety that— when Darby declined to use George Payne— Bill arranged for April to have a bit part, so that someone he knew would be with him on set in the event of a catastrophe. His motivation provides a chilling and damning look at the state of sex work circa the mid-1980s: "At least if I was found dead or mutilated maybe she'd whisper it in someone's ear, and perhaps George would repeat it to other performers, who'd then know to avoid Darby. They always train you not to go to the police in the sex business. If I did get killed, what could April do? Show up at the stationhouse and incriminate herself as a prostitute and accessory to a crime?"

Rather than the start of a new chapter in his porn career, the shoot proved to be the beginning of its end:

"When the nightmare ended I was back in Manhattan and high out of my mind for several days," he wrote in "Body for Rent." "I began to black out… My showbiz illusions were permanently shattered… The drug use took its course. The speedballs would provide a glimpse of clarity, helping me realize that the movies were merely photographed acts of prostitution, but at the same time put a tourniquet on my emotions."

Bill needed to feel in control of his own body, a need that pornography fulfilled, if even only briefly—"The only sense of power I felt was a vicarious power over other men unable to live up to my image. A hollow victory." When reality set in again, he needed drugs to drown it out, and when the drugs were gone, he needed to go back to set to begin the whole vicious cycle over again. Subtly telling about Bill's frame of mind during this period is his photo in the *Rolling Stone* article—looking emaciated in a Seruchi jacket, novelty t-shirt, and skinny jeans, visibly stoned and clutching what appears to be a bag of Chinese takeout, he's a far cry from the healthy, coat-and-tie clad scholar who'd begun documenting 42nd only four years earlier. The caption: "Deep into the Deuce Lifestyle." His life was spiraling out of control, and, like so many sufferers of mental illness, the idea of asking for help was completely out of the question.

As Landis' relationship with George Payne remained consistent, his partnership with Jimmy McDonough was quickly deteriorating, both due to his drug use and his appropriation of *Sleazoid* funds to support his addiction. Soon, McDonough was going out of pocket to pay printing fees. Bill had become a wreck. A supposed Mondo film screening at Danceteria featuring speeches from John Waters, Joel Reed, and Kenneth Anger—the latter of whom Bill had enjoyed an on-again, off-again friendship with since writing about him in the early 80s—fell apart when Bill began advertising it as a "benefit party" for himself and collecting $5 a head and refusing to pay the speakers, leading to an altercation with Anger. Waters, the consummate pro, went onstage and spoke anyway; as an anonymous friend recalls, Bill and Waters had maintained a close friendship up until he began filming porn, a career choice that Waters tried to talk him out of: ""They were friends. John Waters was a fan of *Sleazoid*. At one time Bill had gone down to visit him in Baltimore… They were just friends, there was nothing beyond a friendship between them. But they had a falling out when Bill got into porn. John said 'You really shouldn't do this, this is not a good thing for you to do.' John saw in Bill someone who could really have some mainstream potential, who could make something of himself. But they had a falling out when Bill got into porn and John told him this was a mistake and he shouldn't do it. I know Bill trashed John quite a bit, in subsequent interviews over the years or talked disparagingly about his career, that he'd gone mainstream."

McDonough would later recall to Szpunar the night he entered Bill's apartment to find his blood splattered across the cover of a Lou Reed record left on the floor after a botched hypodermic session (specifically *The Blue Mask*)—an incident that convinced him both *Sleazoid* as a magazine and Bill as a human being were coming to their respective ends.

Ecco: The Story of a Fake Man on 42nd Street was the title Jimmy McDonough gave to the final issue of *Sleazoid*, and it was an appropriate note for the first run of the publication to go out on. More properly called a novella than a magazine, it's an astounding piece of fiction centered on the rise, decline, and fall of Joe Monday—an alias Bill had taken to using as his literary *nom de porn* for sex work-related articles in *Sleazoid*, both paying homage to his Bobby Spector persona and making it appear as though the magazine had an extra contributor. A thinly veiled *roman a clef* about Bill's life on 42nd Street and the psychological and physical rigors of his porn career and drug addiction, *Ecco* is a tour de force of grindhouse literature, effortlessly shifting between gut-busting humor (Joe prides himself on having "been in thirty movies and come in every one of them," and likens himself to a sort of pornographic Superman who charges onto film sets already erect when other men fail to perform), startling ethnographic character sketches (the opening chapter is a Hemmingway-esque cataloging of various individuals on 42nd and what's led them to their current state of ennui) and somber, elegiac contemplation ("One of the greatest pieces of writing I ever laid eyes on," says *Happyland* zine founder Mike McPadden, who spoke to me about his experiences with Bill shortly before his own death in 2020).

While the story retains a sort of tone of manic glee throughout, the subject matter subtly moves from the comic to the tragic. This is perhaps best typified in *Ecco's* standout sequence, in which Joe Monday, desperate for drugs, ends up spending a quiet, almost domestic evening at home with a drug connection, watching television with her and her young son until the boy falls asleep; afterwards, Joe watches over the boy while she goes out to score, only for one of Joe's contact lenses to pop out when he attempts to shoot up after she returns. Hallucinating that Joe's eye has just come out, the horrified woman kicks him out of her apartment, sans contact, forcing him to stumble around with one eye shut until he can obtain an eye patch that he wears home. This fusion of low comedy and somber human drama creates a jarring juxtaposition as *Ecco* enters its final chapter, which finds a delirious Joe shooting up speedballs while listening to the Unifics' "This is the Beginning of My End;" in a fine piece of dramatic irony, readers are well aware by this point that Joe is the nameless "quiet man" whose childhood and premature death from heart failure in the balcony of a Times Square theater are documented in the second chapter. In between, *Ecco* offers insights on the mentality of the various men who flock to Times Square in general and its porn films specifically—"eccos" or "fake men." Joe assesses them as a largely homophobic, ultra-macho lot incapable of properly engaging with their own emotions and unable to express their sexuality—particularly anything other than heteronormative, white-codified sexuality—in any meaningful way. Writing in 1985, his ultimate psychological breakdown nominally describes what we would recognize today as toxic masculinity. It's a work that's at once ahead of its time and deeply tragic in retrospect, especially given McDonough's mission statement: believing that Bill would soon die, he wanted to memorialize both his friend and the circumstances of his demise.

"He went down the mousehole," Keith Crocker says. "He traveled to places other people didn't. He really wanted to live the life, it was something he fully took to his bosom. And of course it's destructive, it's a destructive lifestyle and you'll ultimately end up that way, especially if you're addictive and have that problem. And that's what happened, that's what it was. It was a lifestyle he wanted, but it was also a lifestyle that ate him up."

"Substance abusers aren't fun," says Greg Goodsell. "It's a very claustrophobic, limited life and it's dark. A lot of young men naively think that being a junkie is like walking along the edge and rebellious, and it isn't. You're a slave to something that doesn't give you any pleasure anymore."

At the age of twenty-six, Bill Landis at last burned out— at least temporarily. Porn and drugs had taken their toll on his body and his mind. His relationship with McDonough was no longer sustainable, and, without that moderating force (and someone sober and responsible enough to keep the presses running), *Sleazoid* died a quiet and dignified death with *Ecco*, after five years and forty-eight issues.

A year later, in 1986, Bill finally got the wakeup call he needed, ODing and nearly dying after he bilked a filmmaker out of $100 following a disastrous rooftop porn shoot. "I did a roller-coaster of drugs--black-market methadone, IV speedballs, codeine, and Valium. This binge started as a celebration; fuck-you to a job I hated. In the end it almost killed me." Bill's unlikely hero emerged in the form of George Payne, who saved his life, and offered him what would turn out to be sage—and prophetic—advice:

"Find yourself a girl and quit the business."

Bill did both; and if Bobby Spector and Joe Monday had made their final curtain calls, that girl was about to help set the stage for the return of Mr. Sleazoid…

4.MRS. SLEAZOID

Didn't your mother ever tell you
that you shouldn't go out with
strange men?.

Fleshpot On 42nd Street

As he entered the latter half of the 1980s, Bill Landis found himself faced with two choices: get clean or die. While he would later recount how it was the twin forces of AIDS and crack that ultimately destroyed the 42nd Street he held so dear, Bill himself was facing different demons: intravenous drug addiction compounded by much deeper seated emotional and psychological issues. While Bill may not have realized it at the time, he'd already been offered an unexpected helping hand in the form of a young woman with her own interesting history, one that would leave her uniquely equipped to deal with Bill where others couldn't—and help to pull him out of the abyss when he proved incapable of making the journey himself.

Michelle Clifford was no stranger to the environs Bill was writing about when she first read about *Sleazoid* Express in *Rolling Stone* while laying low down in Florida—"laying low" being the operative words. Clifford's mother was a madame with loose affiliations to Boston's Irish Mafia back in the Winter Hill Gang, Whitey Bulger days. "She was a tough, Irish, mick criminal. *Reservoir Dogs* style… Violent crime and killings... I saw one once, at six years old," Clifford would later recall to Jan Bruun.

While Bill's introduction to vice had come only in his late adolescence, it was an environment in which Clifford had come of age, with pimps, gangsters, and street walkers as her makeshift extended family and guardians. Disaffected prostitutes told her "bedtime stories" involving the robbery of johns and other acts of violence. While Bill was *watching* exploitation movies, Clifford's childhood *was* one, with regular visits to Boston's notorious Combat Zone (the city's analogue to The Deuce), where she saw *Taxi Driver* as a child. It was a sort of gangland fairytale of an adolescence, until the story ended—her mother was shot in the head by the police and Clifford found herself hanging out in libraries down in Florida, away from the heat and scrutiny of a city that had gotten too real, too quick. It was there that she got her first glimpse of Bill's writing, documenting the same environment she'd come of age in, in much the same academic terms she herself used to analyze and critique vice culture in her own burgeoning writing career. She was immediately enthralled—by his world, by his perspective, and by his narrative voice. The two struck up a correspondence, with Landis offering up his encouragement and swapping stories with Clifford; the reader/editor relationship soon developed into one of mentor/mentee, and, in short order, romantic undertones evolved. Bill was twenty-six and, from the outside, nearing the end of his life; Clifford was nineteen and just starting hers'. Did she want to move to New York and get a glimpse of the fabled Deuce firsthand?

Hell, yes, she did.

Clifford arrived in a New York on the brink. It was less than a decade away from the reforms, demolitions, and initiatives that would transform Times Square into the tourist oasis it is today. "[Bill] picked me up from the airport and [we were] inseparable ever since," Clifford later recalled to Clayton Patterson. "My first step in NYC was on 42 Street after taking the shuttle bus from the airport in Jersey." The same day, the pair went on their first date—to the Deuce, of course, for a double feature of *Mountainside Motel Massacre* and *Girls for Sale*. It was a match made in grindhouse heaven.

The circumstances of much of the next few years are known only to Bill and Michelle; Ms. Clifford did not respond to a request for comment. What happened next can only be extrapolated from the aftermath, context clues from subsequent interviews, and brief snippets offered by those few surviving souls who both knew Bill and Michelle and are willing to talk about them. What is certain is that, with Clifford's help, Bill managed to finally kick his speedball habit. The man who'd appeared on the verge of death only a year prior suddenly had a new lease on life, and he had Clifford to thank for it. Over the course of the latter-half of the 80s, an altogether different Bill would emerge—one perhaps less public than the one who'd launched *Sleazoid* at the beginning of the decade, but one more quiet, studious, and contemplative; one less afraid to live outside of the spotlight. In his relationship with Clifford, Bill finally found the validation he'd so craved, from someone who had some idea of the world in which he'd grown up and who didn't shrink away from his lurid tales of hustling or sex work. Though he was soon to enter his thirties, with Michelle's influence, Bill Landis at last finally began to grow up; after a brief stint down in Florida for Bill to dry out, the pair returned to New York to briefly live in the Chelsea Hotel before the inveterate city-dweller got a house in the New Jersey suburbs and returned to 9-5 work in IT and computer programming.

"Michelle's part of the reason that Bill becomes—I don't want to use the word 'respectable' but, in a way, yes," says Keith Crocker. "Suddenly, he's working regular jobs… Bill was trying to play it straight. She was more interested in playing it straight. If you're going to write a book, write it from memories, not from living that lifestyle. Talk about your past in the past tense. She wanted to live a normal lifestyle. She almost seemed to envy the people with the house and the garden and the dog and the kid. It was something she really wanted because she had come from a dysfunctional background. She seemed to envy wanting this type of thing."

The writing from this period betrays a more introspective, thoughtful Bill, and the beginnings of a more focused, scholarly approach to writing under Michelle's influence are apparent. While Bill had contributed to other outlets during his time with *Sleazoid*, now bereft his own medium, he began to branch out further and earn a number of bylines at established publications. "AIDS Fear Hampers Porno Business" appeared in *Variety*, looking at the impact the AIDS crisis was having on adult theaters in general and those on 8th Avenue specifically, focusing on a projectionist's strike there. "Tromatized," which ran in *Film Comment*, both used Troma as a seedy microcosm of the louche world of exploitation studios and praised it for its preservation efforts in salvaging grindhouse classics. The real standout of this period, though, is "Using and Losing on Times Square," which Landis penned under his Joe Monday pseudonym for *The Village Voice*.

A far cry from the spastic, telegraphic style that defined issues of *Sleazoid* only a few years before, it profiles in somber detail the lives (and, in many cases, impending deaths) of various male sex workers Bill had befriended during his time working the Deuce. Gone are the flippancy and biting sarcasm, the casual acceptance of life and death; while Bill had always taken his scene seriously, he'd often done so with tongue firmly in cheek and a certain gallows humor that helped to take the edge off of the stark brutality that defined life on

42nd Street, particularly for its sex workers. Not so in "Using;" here, Bill becomes the detached but mournful anthropologist, offering up matter-of-fact commentary on the rising threat of crack cocaine and AIDS as well as their victims' sometimes casual acquiescence to the inevitability of their own deaths at the hands of one or both. The figures profiled in "Using" are far from the grindhouse burlesques of *Sleazoid*; there are no mad shitters defecating in the aisles of movie theaters or career-criminal drag queens pickpocketing hapless theatergoers. They're real, suffering human beings, and Bill captures them in all of their depth and complexity, never judging or moralizing, often allowing them to tell their own stories in first-person accounts of their hopes, dreams, fears, and failures. It's an altogether more mature piece of writing than anything he'd ever done in *Sleazoid*, and, in retrospect, looking at he and Clifford's collaborative writing and her own solo efforts, it's hard not to see her influence on Bill. Lacking any real formal training in either creative writing or journalism, he'd never had the benefit of someone helping him to focus and hone his craft. In the sort of ersatz writer's workshop that was he and Clifford's relationship, he now had that opportunity, and the results were astounding.

With Michelle's positive influence, Bill would segue away from the nightmare world of porn that had consumed his twenties. While his name pops up in films released as late as 1989, it's unclear at what point he stopped, and whether any of these appearances were recorded prior to her move to NYC (Landis, in reference to his own career, would later remark that it was a common habit of porn distributors to cut in scenes from older films to create new, "package" films). What's clear is that by the dawn of the 1990s, there was a new Bill Landis—one who could engage with his inner Mr. Sleazoid while living a non-destructive daily life. He resumed "straight" work, while at the same time continuing to cover the rapidly dying Times Square culture in which he'd come of age. His work for *The Village Voice* during this period—under his own name now—is poignant and insightful, including the aforementioned "Body for Rent," in which he essentially retells *Ecco* in his own words and without any playful pseudonyms or comic asides. Now most largely available as an archived copypaste on alt.sex.movies titled simply "Bobby Spector Article," it's a piece of stunningly raw emotional, sexual, and psychological honesty that's almost the direct inverse of the obfuscating punk edge of the old *Sleazoid*. It's in "Rent" that Bill finally addresses in simple but blunt detail his upbringing, sexual assault, complicated adolescence and porn career; the details are explicit but never crude, instead offering the reader an intimate account of his life up to that point, including how Clifford's influence helped pull him back from the brink. It's arguably one of his strongest pieces of non-film-related writing, and one that still resonates today for its fearlessness in addressing the lives and experiences of male sexual abuse survivors—a topic still nominally considered verboten in 2021.

It was far from the only piece of personal writing

Bill would do with Michelle's encouragement. His 1992 essay for *The Village Voice*, "Point of Return," positively examined ACT-UP's needle exchange program, speaking from his own personal experience as an IV drug user. The piece, which advocated providing clean needles to addicts and recovering addicts as a means of curtailing the AIDS crisis, proved to be both a popular and impactful work that reached a wider audience than ever before, being republished in the AIDs-related book *Beyond Crisis* and, more astoundingly, in a widely-disseminated UCLA Handbook. Never before had the subject matter been so timely or relevant, its reach so profound. While this period in Bill's life produced the least amount of material relating to exploitation cinema, it seems, personally, to have been one of his most productive. In addition to his various bylines, he and Clifford were officially married—*twice,* curiously, at least according to official New York City records, which have them tying the knot first in 1991 (marriage license 25687) and again in 1994 (2118), both times in Manhattan (further complicating issues is that Bill's apparently self-penned Encyclopedia.com entry lists their marriage year as 1986).

While Landis' writing—and life—had flourished in the 90s, though, his beloved Deuce was breathing its last. The environment there—as he himself had vaguely alluded to in "Using and Losing"—was unsustainable. What had once been a dangerous playland for vice workers, runaways, and thrill seekers had become a hostile death trap, and both he and the City of New

York knew it. Crackdowns on prostitution and drug dealing led to the inevitable closure of the grindhouses, which had become safe-havens for every stripe of criminal, drug user, and sex worker to use as de facto headquarters or hideouts. To hear Bill and Michelle tell it, the grindhouses officially died in 1993 after the Liberty Theater played *Falling Down*, a tale of moral ambiguity, urban decay, and misguided rage that served as an appropriate last feature for the blighted block. The wrecking balls and developers came in; what surviving denizens of the Deuce were still alive wandered off in search of seedier pastures. As Bill would tell you himself, the rest were dead. Two years later, in 1995, he would contribute to a *Village Voice* article about the "Disneyfication" of 42nd Street, pondering in simultaneous relief and bemusement how an area that had once been so deadly yet full of life could now be so safe and yet so dead.

What was someone so intrinsically *of* The Deuce to do in its absence?

Catalog what was left, Michelle reasoned.

Bill's old frenemy Kenneth Anger was still alive and kicking in the 90s (as he remains as of the writing of this book— now *in* his 90s). He represented for her as much as anyone one of the last vanguards of a lost and forgotten era and ethos. Why not preserve a piece of lost 42nd Street by preserving Anger himself, still alive to tell so many tales? Bill was intrigued by the idea, and, with Michelle's first encouragement and then assistance, embarked on what was then the most ambitious writing project of his career. "Ken Anger had hawked but never completed his own autobio for years in publishing circles," Bill recalled to Patterson. "Michelle really instigated it. When we met, she asked why there wasn't a book about him. She really liked his films tremendously. They were the first art films she ever saw… She had me get an agent and then she wrote half of it, although her name wasn't on it. She did the interviews with Manson associate Bobby Beausoliel for it, amongst other parts."

Published in 1995, *Anger: The Unauthorized Biography of Kenneth Anger* was Bill and Michelle's first substantial collaboration, and remains a highly controversial and fascinating read. Despite the arduous research that went into the book, including Bill's own conversations with Anger, Anger himself fiercely denounced the project, its content, and Bill himself, later claiming to have conducted a magick working to place a Crowelian death curse on him. Although not a major commercial success, the book found its audience among underground movie afficionados and survivors of 42nd Street, drawn by its "look behind the curtain" feel and alternating hero-worship/critical approach to Anger and his work. It was, in a way, the sort of second coming of Mr. Sleazoid—older, wiser, more scholarly and focused, and now part of a double-barreled writing team to be reckoned with. Tellingly, Michelle took on the mantle of "Mrs. Sleazoid," with the couple using the addresses to refer to one another in their collaborative writing. Most importantly, the cult-success of *Anger—*

along with the growing cultural interest in exploitation cinema, now beginning to discover a second life both on the VHS grey market and through more legitimate means such as Something Weird's reissue operation—demonstrated to Mr. and Mrs. Sleazoid that there was still an appetite for information about grindhouse movies and the culture that had birthed them. As the 90s drew to a close, and Bill found himself at a more stable point than any in his life, the stage was set for an event a decade-and-a-half in the making: the return of *Sleazoid Express*.

5. JUPITER AND BEYOND THE INFINITE

Block: *Have you come for me?*
Death: *I have walked at your side for a long time now.*

The Seventh Seal

As the millennium came to a close and a wary America looked forward to the looming Y2K crisis (spoiler: nothing happened), Bill Landis was enjoying one of the most productive, stable, and, arguably, happiest times in his life. He was married to the love of his life; he'd written a book that had enjoyed modest cult success and found its intended audience; and, perhaps most notably, he'd become a father. Victoria Sabine Landis—"Baby Sleazoid"— was born in 1997, a "moon child" by Clifford's description, conceived in accordance with the teachings of German Renaissance philosopher Paracelcus and occultist Aleister Crowley. By all accounts, she was the apple of her father's eye. There's a surreal yet touching humanity to reading Bill's recollections of taking her to the Toys "R" Us in Times Square or out to see the *Thomas the Tank Engine* movie. An altogether more grounded, sentimental, and humble Bill emerges in stories about Victoria, and what little is available regarding their relationship points to an intimate father/daughter bond far removed from the cold, abusive, and loveless parent/child relationship Bill describes having with his own parents (a request for interview sent to Victoria Landis at her last known address did not elicit a response; her current whereabouts are unknown. A blog she briefly operated in the 2000s documenting the Chicago punk scene has since gone offline and only scant posts remain accessible via archive.org). Following in her father's footsteps, those who met her recall Victoria as an incredibly intelligent, inquisitive, linguistically gifted child.

"Really brilliant child," Art Ettinger recalls. "I spent time with the three of them… I was impressed that the child's vocabulary seemed like a young genius' in the making."

By the age of eight, she was capable of holding her own in chess games against adult opponents and was already programming her own website; both parents were proud. Indeed, a story that Ettinger tells about this period in Bill's life paints a picture of a man completely antithetical to the speedball-addicted, porn-star junkie of the 1980s: "Having dinner with him on Christmas Day was really a dream come true for me. He was in a good mood and-- trying to put a word on it-- it was just one of those unreal moments, that you get to spend Christmas with one of your heroes. There was a reciprocal nature to the friendship, meaning he seemed to be happy to be there with us as we were with him. It was fulfilling to me. I was just at the beginning of my genre trajectory, and he was really flattering about *Ultra Violent* magazine, he said things like, 'It's wonderful, you're going to become quite famous for it,' yadda yadda yadda. He was this hyper-verbal, magnetic person to be around. He was fun, he was funny, he was extremely intelligent, and to get to know one of your heroes to that degree. I can't think of a less cliche way of saying it— it's a dream come true."

Going further, Ettinger—who befriended Bill after he and Michelle inquired about reprinting a photo Ettinger had taken of *Last House on Dead End Street* director Roger Watkins with David Hess— offers a Bill Landis even further outside the realm of Mr. Sleazoid: "He was an incredibly verbal individual… a lot of great writers are not necessarily verbal… Bill would use big words in every big conversation, but he was also really quick on his feet, really witty. He had a similar sensibility about film as I do. He was never a 'so bad it's good' type, he was never pointing and laughing at these old exploitation movies; he sort of saw their merits. Of course, there's a lot of ridiculous material out there, we all laugh at it, but he had this great tremendous respect for it... he loved arthouse cinema, and I think that's telling. When you go on a book tour, and you have a chance to show something on 35mm and instead of choosing an Al Adamson flick or a Ted V. Mikels flick, he chose *Nanami*. It's not that obscure, not anymore, because there's a Criterion release of it, but that's a film person's film. The average viewer wouldn't know what sense to make of that piece. That's an arthouse film and indicative of the kind of film that Bill was into. There were certain films he liked; there was this one film, Robert Altman's *That Cold Day in the Park,* that he talked about a lot. He just had certain movies he referenced a lot; he had an encyclopedic knowledge of cinema in general. I think that impressed me too... on the list of things he liked about me, I think he was impressed to find someone my age as well-versed as I am. His generation sees my generation the way my generation sees Millennials, and it can be quite rude and dismissive. He wasn't that way. He was like I see myself when I deal with Millennials: open-minded and hopeful."

Not that domesticity had completely conquered the Landises. You could take Bill out of the Deuce, but you couldn't take the Deuce out of Bill; in addition to contributing to Philadelphia-based genre magazine *Carbon 14,* in 1997 he began contributing to Clifford's newly launched publication *Metasex*. Like *Sleazoid, Metasex* was a DIY publication from the heart, a sort of journal of the vice industry. Ahead of its time, *Metasex* wasn't so much sex positive as it was sex nonjudgmental, examining such topics as S&M, prostitution, pornography, and sex in cinema through an analytical, academic lens. It was the sort of scholarly assessment of sex work and sexuality and their depiction in the media that the current generation of film writers are still struggling to nail down. It's a testament to Michelle's abilities and vision that she conceptualized the project when she did, and to both Bill's belief in her and her mission that he lent his expertise and personal experiences to making the magazine into something more than *Sleazoid* had been. After two years, though, the bug apparently bit; Bill had found himself back in familiar territory. No longer the angry young man of the grindhouse scene, he was—as he entered his forties—something of an elder statesman. He was called up to provide a brief talking head segment on Kenneth Anger in the 1998 John Waters documentary *Divine Trash*. He was more grounded than he'd been the first time he'd seen and written about exploitation movies; he had the perspective and benefit of age; he wasn't spending significant amounts of time hustling for drug money. Weened on worn-out VHSes and third-generation dubs with Romanian subtitles, Quentin Tarantino had introduced an entirely new generation to the very concept of grindhouse cinema, and early-aughts America was hungry for more information on an era of cinematic innovation that'd been lost to them by virtue of time, drugs, disease, and urban redevelopment. American culture was hungry to walk the Deuce, if only in spirit, and Bill Landis was in a prime position to act as their tour guide. In 1999, he and Michelle made the decision to relaunch *Sleazoid Express.*

Originally intended as a sort of "getting the band back together" endeavor, Bill reached out to Jimmy McDonough, wanting to bring him back on board for *Sleazoid* 2.0. McDonough was more than reluctant, feeling that they'd "shot their wad" on the first iteration of the magazine, preferring to leave it as a sacrosanct time capsule of a special era in their lives and in cinema history. His refusal to join the new staff marked the final falling out between the sporadic collaborators; Bill was apoplectic that McDonough wouldn't return. Two years later, McDonough would both pay tribute to Bill for his influence and acknowledge the end of their relationship in his book *The Ghastly One*, a biography of Andy Milligan. "For Landis—Arrividerci," McDonough wrote in the dedication, a line that's only become more haunting with the passage of time. "It was a big surprise when I started doing things on my own, let me tell you. It never would've happened at all if it hadn't been for Landis," McDonough told Szpunar. "And that's why *The Ghastly One* is dedicated to him... that one's for Bill."

Never one to let enemies or hurdles—real or imagined—get in his way, Bill soldiered on, with Michelle assuming McDonough's old role as his muse, collaborator, and cheerleader. New issues of *Sleazoid* rolled off the presses in 1999, just in time for the new millennium. Whereas a certain terseness had characterized the original run of the magazine, *Sleazioid* 2.0 was a more contemplative endeavor, less concerned with telegraphic, gonzo recollections of films and filmgoers and more focused on the examination of exploitation cinema from a more disciplined anthropological perspective. Gone were the paragraph-long, stream-of-consciousness reviews; in their place were pages-long discussions of textual themes, analyses of the socio-political environs that had birthed particular films, and those films' place within the sociological cinematic canon of their age. While several avowed fans of the first run of *Sleazoid* have criticized the revival for lacking in the *je ne sais quoi* of its progenitor, the second life of the zine is inarguably more polished, coherent, and critically satisfying from a textual perspective. The double-barrel of Bill's more grounded perspective and Michelle's own influence and contributions coalesced to make it a more insightful and thoughtful product than the first run. Readers concerned with style over substance may have argued that the flash and provocation were gone, but, they remained, albeit hidden beneath a veneer of respectability and panache (issues of the new *Sleazoid* topped out at 70 pages, versus the one-sheet it'd begun life as). At a time when genre journalism was still nominally concerned with BTS SFX articles, gossip, and giving front cover space to whatever studio paid the most money, *Sleazoid* was delving into themes of social justice, systemic racism, the depiction of sexual abuse in the media, and innumerable other subjects it would take another two decades for the major publications to begin seriously addressing. Arguably, without the second coming of *Sleazoid,* there's no modern iterations of *Rue*

Morgue, Fangoria, or *Diabolique,* the first two of which only more recently began the sociocultural analyses they've come to be known for.

The resurgence of the magazine didn't go unnoticed; the exploitation cinema the Landises loved so much was enjoying a second life as the reissue houses began to re-release old Deuce standbys, the first such opportunity for many of these films. The surviving members of the old guard wanted to relive the bad old days, rediscover lost classics, and get a look at stuff they'd missed during the first run; Gen-Xers and Xennials were embracing a lost era they'd just barely missed out on being a part of. Clifford had long encouraged Landis to see to it that his work was not only preserved for posterity but joined the ranks of Kerouac and Boroughs as pop culture canon. "When we met, she said I needed a mass market flexi-book that was affordable and would be under every college kid's bong by their VCR," Bill recalled to Patterson.

"I wouldn't let Times Square die without a proper funeral," Michelle added. "I wanted permanent books. So everyone could learn what hath occurred."

So it was that the pair signed a book deal with Simon and Schuster, and, in December of 2002, *Sleazoid Express: A mind Twisting Tour Through the Grindhouse Cinema of Times Square* was released for mass consumption. It was part of a zeitgeist; 2003 was, in a way, the year that grindhouse finally went authentically mainstream after a decade of soft-pedaled allusions. *Jackie Brown* may have given a respectful ode to the blaxploitation cinema of yesteryear and *Pulp Fiction* may have been something of a spiritual successor to old-school expy cinema, but '03 was the year that filmmakers stopped winking and nodding and started offering up their own sincere entries in the exploitation canon. It was the year that saw the release of *Kill Bill,* Tarantino's homage to the chop socky and low-rent action films he'd come of age on; it was also the year that Rob Zombie dropped *House of 1000 Corpses* on a largely confused and off-put audience who may have more readily understood--and embraced—the film if, like loyal *Sleazoid* readers, they understood the cinematic tradition that it was following in. As seemingly every genre director began producing their own self-described "grindhouse" films, Bill and Michelle were there to set the record straight on who had it right, who had it egregiously wrong, and what it all meant in the first place.

The *Sleazoid* book is something of the apotheosis of all of Bill's writing on the Deuce and exploitation cinema, and, if one can't ever get their hands on anything else he ever committed to the page, it's a perfect tome for understanding not only its subject matter but the man who co-wrote it. Taking the form of a tour of 42nd Street, the book explores a variety of subgenres of exploitation cinema via the theaters that specialized in them. The chapter "Bloodthirsty Butchers at the Lyric," for example, not only explores the history of the eponymous theater but also delves into the career of Bill's beloved Andy Milligan, whose films were a staple there. "The Anco Does a Gender Twist" recalls the heyday of that theater and the sexploitation and early trans-cinema movies that made it famous. From the book's fascinating introductory chapter, which gives a brief history of what made the Deuce what it was and the fate that befell it, to the elegiac and bittersweet climax "Lost at the Roxy" (in which Michelle gets the final word, offering a poetic ode to both 42nd and her own time there), the *Sleazoid* book is a masterpiece of journalism, ethnography, and film study; it remains a piece of required reading for every college junior with a camera who thinks that their "ironic" screenplay about street-racing werewolf gangsters is "authentic grindhouse." Every page drips with love and remembrance, and the critical analysis on display here is more refined, poignant, on-key and revelatory than anything Bill had ever committed to the page before. He and Clifford demonstrate themselves the perfect writing team, with her contributions and influence elevating the *Sleazoid* subject matter beyond everything that had come before. It will be an eternal shame that it was the only book on exploitation cinema the pair ever wrote; but, if there could only be one, the world of cinema studies will forever be indebted to the Landises that it was *this* book.

While the *Sleazoid* book wasn't a runaway success, it developed an even more prominent cult following than *Anger*. The Landises soon found themselves the guests of honor and masters of ceremonies at a variety of film festivals, movie screenings, and special events throughout the country, making such journeys to Chicago's Music Box Theater and Austin's Alamo

Drafthouse to introduce and host Q&As on exploitation classics. It was the life Bill had always dreamed of back in his 14th street days, only now someone was doing the distribution work for him. Now, all he had to do was show up with his wife and partner in crime, receive the applause, and bask in the adoration afforded to them as the elder statesmen of the grindhouse scene.

It should have been something of a fairy tale ending—the brilliant but tragic young scribe finding salvation from his demons through the love of his artistic and intellectual equal, the pair blazing a trail in the field of their shared fascination. As Jimmy McDonough so thoughtfully put it to Szpunar, though, "Bill was a walking exploitation movie"—and as any expy fan knows, these stories rarely have happy endings.

At some point, Bill had lapsed back into drug use—his substance of choice now: opioids. In a chilling prefiguration of the crisis that would sweep America in the coming decades, Bill wrote at length about the benefits of cheap and easy access to opioids in a 2003 *Village Voice* article entitled "Go Email the Doctor," extolling the virtues of online pharmacies while decrying the predatory and often ineffective nature of health insurance companies and their concern with bilking patients out of the largest amount of money possible, regardless of actual care. On the surface, it's a brave and relevant condemnation of America's still broken healthcare system; reading the piece with the knowledge of Bill's problem, though, it takes on a much more sinister undercurrent.

Ostensibly written from an objective perspective, Bill's detached tales of fruitless appointments with pain management clinics, mounting medical bills, and frustration with being ping-ponged to multiple doctors betray that he's really trying to tell the reader about his own struggles, albeit in ellipticals. Tellingly, the article cites a rib injury as an example of something for which an apathetic doctor may only prescribe Advil, when, in Bill's opinion, opioid painkillers would be more justified. He makes a similar reference to the need for pain pills to treat a rib injury in his Joel Reed *Sleazoid* issue, claiming it was just such an injury that led to his speedball habit in the 80s. It's hard not to read *Email* now and not see it as a professionally written and published apologia for opioid abuse. While the explicit thesis of the article is the need for healthcare reform as regards pain treatment and management, a second, more insidious point emerges by article's end: I am an addict and this is why.

"There were issues with addiction," Keith Crocker recalls. "He went from job to job. I don't think there was anything he had that was long term. Part of this is the problem of Bill Landis and relationships. I don't think that 'long term' was meant for Bill. Bill was flying by the seat of his pants, and as soon as something started to get dull or get to the point where it relied on him too much, he would dodge it. That's what I personally believe."

If the period between the end of the first *Sleazoid* and its revival are cloudy due to their mundanity, the years following the publication of the *Sleazoid* book are vague because of their chaos and tragedy. Few of the living want to openly discuss their misfortune; few friends of the dead wish to speak ill of their loved ones' final, unhappy years. Michelle Clifford wanted to be a writer married to a writer, working together to express their mutual artistic endeavors; she didn't want to be married to a drug addict. Only Bill Landis could ever say for sure what the source of his addiction was. Perhaps it truly was purely physical (those cracked ribs come up again), and he really was a casualty of a healthcare system content to throw dangerous drugs at patients and usher them out of the office in exchange for a quick insurance payment. Maybe he never really did get over the crippling emotional and sexual trauma that defined his early years. It could have been the stress of the sudden, unexpected success that befell him later in life; maybe it was some deep-seated, dark, and secret pain that only Bill could ever truly know.

Whatever it was, in rapid succession, the Landises' life began to fall apart. The final years of their marriage are a mélange of last-chance grasps for salvation and struggles to make it work. The Joel Reed *Sleazoid* issue, published in 2005, points to early cracks in their relationship, with the mournful dedication "I still love you, Michelle – Bill xxxxoooo." Tellingly, unlike previous collaborative efforts, Michelle does not offer a reciprocal dedication. Rather, Bill is left alone to fall back on an old narrative conceit paying tribute to his love of rock and roll, addressing an imaginary disc jockey and requesting "Mr. DJ – Please play 'If Lovin' You is Wrong I Don't Wanna Be Right' and 'Wild Horses' for Michelle from Bill." Particularly in light of the pair's dedications to one another at the beginning of the *Sleazoid* book only a few years before, the dissolution is tragic: "In homage to your sexy genius, let me spin some tunes of tribute," Michelle wrote in the book. "The velour 'Juicy' by M'Tume and a raunchy song, 'Live With Me' by the Stones. For my hardworking Sleazoid loverman and scholar." Bill returns the favor a few lines later: "You've been my perfect writing partner. You are the still waters I was always seeking, spiritually and aesthetically… In homage to both your irresistible charisma and beauty and your instinctive understanding of Times Square: Hey Mr. DJ, please play 'Ain't No Stoppin' Us Now' by McFadden and Whitehead. Love always, Bill"

The songs may have remained the same but the marriage was crumbling. While Michelle had been able to help him get clean in the past, there was a child in the picture now; the pair were older, and this wasn't punk-rock Regan-era Times Square anymore. After having tasted the legitimacy of suburban domesticity, Michelle no longer had any patience for Bill's worsening addiction. The pair briefly moved to Florida to be near Bill's parents in an effort to make it work in a new environment, with help from grandma and grandpa in caring for Baby Sleazoid. The experience proved traumatic for Bill, who later recounted his struggles in a never published spiritual sequel to *Ecco,* titled *Last Exit in Manhattan,* a tour-de-force third-person novella about "Bobby Spector" provided to me by a friend of Bill's who wishes to remain anonymous. Written in the same clipped yet evocative tones of *Ecco, Last Exit* finds Bobby, "Danielle" (Michelle) and "Veronica" (Victoria) traveling South following a spate of bad luck, including an apartment fire and the socioeconomic depression brought on by 9/11. Hoping for a fresh start, Bill and Michelle published the sixth issue of the new *Sleazoid* there, but otherwise the period proved creatively fruitless.

"Bobby became involved in the internet pill companies that emanated out of the area," Landis writes of his time in a part of Florida he disparagingly refers to as "The Redneck Riviera." "Apart from his role as a quasi-consultant, web copywriter, market researcher and full time addict for one particular firm, he retreated from life in general. The suburbs, nosy hillbillies by a pool, and the heat were not his speed. He had never fit in in Florida— and never would. This area was more irritating, uptight and obnoxious than his last stay in Miami/Fort Lauderdale years back. Had he been cold stone sober he would have still hated everyone's guts."

Deciding that a return to the Northeast was the only solution to his worsening psychological state, Landis went back to New York sans Michelle and Victoria, moving in with an old Avon theater associate until he could find a place for the family to make a fresh start. Fatefully, the place Bill finally settled on was a derelict apartment in Washington Heights, soon to be of Lin Manuel Miranda *In the Heights* fame. Still an epicenter of narcotics and gang violence in 2005, it proved to be the only location the Landises could afford. Following a detailed prologue documenting the ethnographic history of the Heights dating back to the 1920s, culminating in a gang war between Puerto Ricans and Dominicans in which the Dominicans ultimately emerged victorious (the best outcome, per Bill, a lifelong lover of Dominican culture and food), *Last Exit* finds Bill, Michelle, and Victoria beginning an uncertain new life back in New York, as one of the sole non-Latin families in the neighborhood. Despite their outsider status, the family found themselves welcomed by their new neighbors; boys doted on Victoria, whom they nicknamed "Blonde Princess" and "Supergirl," while Bill became something of an unofficial OG, recognized by the drug lords who ran their apartment building as an aging addict with life experience under his belt.

Though they struggled with an apathetic super and occasional nosy neighbors, the Landises settled into something approximating normalcy in 2005; nonetheless, Bill was apprehensive about the environment into which he'd brought his family. "Ghetto living had never helped Bobby's mindset," he writes in *Last Exit*. "Despite the considerable knowledge about human nature he had gained from it, he'd always wound up an insider in questionable gray areas but at great cost to his own psyche and physicality. He didn't want his girls dragged into this scene." While Bill's 1980s *Sleazoid* writing had betrayed a certain jadedness, *Last Exit* drips with raw, aching humanity, as he worries for his wife and daughter's future in a drug inundated neighborhood, where windows are regularly shattered by bullet holes and Victoria witnesses a man loading a gun in their stairwell. Due to strict geographical constraints, Victoria is unable to enroll in a prestigious art school only blocks away from their apartment; addicts press their buzzer at all hours, mistaking their apartment for a drug den; Bill worries what will happen as his daughter comes of age, concerned that she'll become the girlfriend or mistress of a burgeoning drug lord. Surprisingly, *Last Exit* also documents the formerly atheistic Bill's apparent conversion to Catholicism, as he begins attending the historic Church of the Incarnation. Though he had (apparently jokingly) once referred to his religion as "Thelemite," *Last Exit* finds a devout Landis attending mass to pray for the salvation of his marriage, even bringing along Michelle and Victoria. "The Church of the Incarnation had been something of a refuge for Bobby," Bill writes. "He could sit there and cry at a pew. No one would make fun or think it odd, not even the most macho character. No one knew his problem or the gravity of it. It just *was*. People had serious problems that came in that church – their health could be failing… their kid could have OD'd…. so no one found his behavior peculiar. Parishioners would touch the religious icons and pray to them, douse themselves in holy water before and after leaving it." Later, in an even greater show of devotion, Bill describes himself visiting a *botánica,* where he professes a dedication to the Saints and—describing his marital and addiction woes to a sympathetic *santerio*— agrees to pray for his own salvation. For the formerly acerbic and disaffected punk-chronicler of 42nd Street, it's in these moments of raw spirituality that Landis' vulnerability most shines through.

Even more strikingly, *Last Exit* contains some of Bill's most insightful self-reflection, psychoanalyzing himself as someone prone to putting up walls even when emotional intimacy would be the healthier route: "In his unemotional stupor he showed no resistance," Bill writes of his deepening fear for his family. "But Bobby was not the emotional type to begin with, both a defense mechanism he developed as a young adult after too many encounters with neurotic New York women and a trait he had learned as a young adult from his mentor George Payne about never to appear emotionally dependent on anyone. This coldness often proved his downfall in close interpersonal relationships, especially those needing any reciprocal affection."

That coldness would prove to be the downfall of his marriage. After some time in The Heights, the unthinkable happened: Michelle packed Victoria up and headed for a new life—sans Bill—in Chicago. Left to his own devices, Bill—struggling to find and keep employment as a temp worker— became something of an unofficial member of the gang running his apartment building, allowing dealers to use his place to sell cocaine and serving as a lookout when police made routine checks of the area, once being pulled over and questioned himself. Too, Bill became the quasi-mentor of a burgeoning young crime lord, whose awkward devotion he spends much of *Last Exit* trying to understand, questioning if the young man's interest is romantic, platonic, or even if the boy had come of age watching his Bobby Spector films, which had become objects of cult fascination amongst 42nd Street's Hispanic/Latino community twenty years before, due to Bill's ambiguous ethnicity. "Bobby thought, yeah, it would be a freaky, one of a kind, one-shot experience," Bill muses of a potential romantic entanglement. "Bobby was a self-aware pervert and there were few things he hadn't done. Out of all his numerous encounters prior to his marriage there were none with a Dominican gang member. But then what would result?" Ultimately deciding the potential fallout could be disastrous, Bill opted not to pursue the relationship any further.

Bill's close ties to the drug community would prove fortuitous when— returning home one Winter night while high following a brief period of sobriety— he blacked out trying to open his front door, resulting in his falling and shattering his arm in two places. Nearly freezing to death, he was saved by a high-ranking gang member who recognized him and called an ambulance. A period of involuntary commitment followed, as the drug-addled, paranoid, and vindictive Bill was deemed to be a threat to himself. With Michelle still in Chicago, Bill's care fell to his agent, Janet Rosen, who made regular trips to the asylum to check in on him and counsel him that his own hostile attitude was keeping him committed. Despite her admonitions to act rational with the staff,

Bill's ongoing combativeness resulted in his being kept hospitalized for some time (it was during this period that Joel Reed claims he had his final conversation with Bill, described as a collect call he placed from one of the asylum's payphones). It was also during this period that the doctors' routine checks indicated to Bill that his health was failing: a self-admitted heavy smoker, X-rays displayed what appeared to be a spot on his lung; he was suffering from liver poisoning; and he was also diagnosed with a urinary tract infection, a triumvirate of ailments that disturbed him. "Bobby eventually said that it was a wake-up call to watch his health, and he had allowed himself to get too run down," Bill writes in *Last Exit*. Ultimately released, Bill returned to The Heights ever more galvanized against straight society, and further enshrined himself with the gang to the point that they began providing him with free drugs in exchange for his services as a lookout and the use of his apartment to conduct deals.

While his life was spiraling out of control, there were periods of hope and stability throughout 2005. It was during this time that Bill met Swedish journalist, photographer, and filmmaker Carl Abrahamsson, who took some of the last known photos of Bill and conducted one of his final interviews, which Bill characterizes in *Last Exit* as "one of his most honest and forthcoming." Although *Sleazoid* was petering out, Landis took the opportunity to deliver what could be seen as the publication's manifesto and a summation of everything he and Michelle tried to accomplish: "With both *Sleazoid* and *Metasex*, we wanted to kink everything up. We had some competition, some imitators. We were trying to go into the unspeakable. The fourth [new] *Sleazoid* had the sadism picture from *Performance* on the cover. There was a bit of Karin Schubert history. I believe that art and exploitation is the same thing. There's no distinction between them for me. For me, an Ingmar Bergman movie is the same as an exploitation movie that's sexually oriented. Every movie is a work of art."

"For me it was very cool to actually meet him because he was very much like I had envisioned him in a way," Abrahamsson recalls. "This happened in 2005. That was a period where I had delved into other things because this love of weird films. You can never leave it. It's there all along. And it didn't take much scratching on my surface to get back into that scene and romanticizing a part of New York that is forever gone, for good or bad I don't know. But Bill was there in the aftermath and managed to convey what it was like and it was very, very thrilling to meet that person who had been there and experienced those things. Intellectually he was very sharp. He was completely aware of what he had done and what he had in terms of knowledge and capacity, and I could feel he was very proud about the Kenneth Anger book.... At the same time there was a slight tinge of bitterness. He had hoped for things to be even better. But on the whole a very vital mind. Metabolically a different story. He was worn down. You could see that physically... But it didn't really affect anything. We just had a great time talking. That chemical allure was part and parcel of the old environment. Some people who had worked in adult entertainment as it's now called, maybe they could leave it with 'I had a great time, I made some money, goodbye, good riddance.' Many people were, and I think still are, dented. They become dented in their general persona. It's not for everyone. I think that was the main thing— having gone from being this romantic young guy, even as a teenager, and then going into that world. That's a dividing line, where you're either a passionate consumer or you become someone involved in the lifestyle. We talked about that. He was dented by those years. I don't claim to know him well, maybe there were other things in his personal life that helped this addiction, because he'd also written a lot about drugs. So I don't know if that was a justification, dealing with your own addiction by writing about it and making it not as threatening as it is. He was completely functional, super sharp, a charming guy. I've met many, many people who are chemically challenged, and very few of them have been real assholes or deadbeats. Most of them can function really well but that doesn't mean you want to live with them 24/7. When we were done, we went to have a drink at some bar close by. He was so happy to get this kind of attention..." Too, Bill found himself developing a friendship with a local UPS employee he names "Maria" in *Last Exit,* who allowed him to use the store's computers and copier for free and who developed a flirtation with him. Wanting to remain faithful to Michelle, he turned down her advances, though—in one of the most vulnerable confessions of

Last Exit—he admits he tried to get her to attend Easter mass with him at The Church of the Incarnation.

Ultimately, life alone in The Heights became too much for Bill. After a SWAT raid on his apartment building in which several of his drug associates were arrested, it came time to consider a move; Michelle had expressed her willingness to attempt a reconciliation, but only if Bill came to Chicago. The time had come for the consummate New Yorker to say a final goodbye to the environment that had shaped and defined him, and whose culture and transformation he had done so much to document. The final paragraph of *Last Exit* finds a restless Bill on the eve of his departure bidding a final farewell to his beloved Big Apple: "After listening to the do-wop shop on New York's oldies station, CBS-FM, the last night grew so unbearable that he actually called the Dominican cabbie three hours before his flight at La Guardia. Driving on the street he saw two white males aggressively wandering around at 2:30 a.m. One looked very much like Bobby in his deteriorated, vice world, plastic purple Serucchi jacket stage in the mid-1980s. A very *Roman Spring of Mrs. Stone* moment indeed, like when the Warren Beatty character sees versions of him who have fallen onto very hard times. The driver just said, 'You don't see people like that downtown…'"

Thus ends one of Bill's final pieces of writing, and the last honest, autobiographical work of his life.

2006 found Bill in Chicago, living apart from Michelle but attempting to restore his marriage and rebuild his career as an elder statesman of the grindhouse scene. His public appearances in this period are chillingly familiar for those who knew him during the depths of his speedball dependence; the quiet, more somber Bill of the 90s and of *Last Exit* gave way to the raging inferno of paranoia, obsessive vindictiveness, and indignity that had defined his Bobby Spector era in the 1980s.

"I had some freelance work at *Celebrity Skin*, so I offered it to them," said Mike McPadden. Bill "felt like they didn't get paid fast enough. This was a peril of writing for any magazine back in the early 2000s. It could take up to six months and a lot of reminding payroll department before you got paid for freelance. That's just the way it was. So Bill began his terror campaign. And I heard his voice..." At this point, McPadden— as virtually everyone who knew Bill will do when remembering him— slipped into an imitation of Bill's distinct *New Yawkese*: "'*Listen, this isn't funny anymore. I know terrorist techniques! I can bankrupt your company and ruin their credit rating just with prank phone calls'* [a reference to Bill's knowledge of phone phreaking]. I started getting Satanic post cards in the mail and things like that.... I wasn't really scared, but it was an enormous pain in my ass. I was some fucking two-bit jerk-off working for *Celebrity Skin* magazine and it was like, [Bill's voice] '*You're the managing ed-it-or. Do something!*' There was nothing I *could* do. Finally, I got them paid."

Bill's crumbling life was only confirmed later for McPadden when the two had an opportunity to meet face-to-face in Chicago, following the Landises' flight there. The story of those encounters paints in vivid detail the mindset of Bill's final days:

"Rocco Malce, who published *Claw Hold* magazine, brought Bill to Quimby's. It was a big deal. I'm finally gonna match a face to this voice. So, they have this event, Rocco's there, I brought all my friends, at least ten people. And there were two goth girls there and like nobody else, but it looked like a pretty good crowd. And I see this little wormy guy with a fanny pack smoking foot-long cigarettes, just reading from old *Sleazoid Expresses*. And it's completely bizarre. So I said to him—I did not identify myself, and I was a little bit of a shit disturber, but not entirely— I said, 'Would you ever work with Jimmy McDonough again?' He goes, [Bill voice] *'No! FUCK no! I heard he dedicated a book to me. Fuck him!'* He had a complete meltdown. He goes, *'Let me tell you something about Jimmy McDonough, let me tell you. Jimmy McDonough likes to photograph his girlfriend in lesbian situations.'* First of all, I don't think that's true. Second of all, is that scandalous to anybody?"

As in the Joel Reed Issue of *Sleazoid,* Bill's drug-addled mind had begun concocting outlandish scenarios about the people he believed to have crossed him, with McPadden himself remembering in the midst of the Quimby's debacle how he'd been on the receiving end himself: "In the middle of the madness of Bill bombarding me wanting to get paid- and he was right to want to get paid— he'd said to me, 'I know who you are!' Now, I published *Happyland* under the name Selwyn

Harris, which were the last two grindhouse theaters on 42nd Street, the Selwyn and the Harris. He said, [Bill voice] *'I know who you are, Selwyn Harris. I know all about you and the two dominatrixes in the deli.'* And I was like—first off, whatever he was thinking in his head, I *wish* it were true! It sounds like the coolest story ever. I mean, I had dominatrix friends. We might've wandered into a deli at some point to buy a beer or a coffee, but, I can tell you assuredly there was no colorful story attached to that. So who knows what he was thinking? This was… what do you call it? The orgy of a sick mind, to use a bootleg video title of *Bloodsucking Freaks*."

Fascinated to see more of Bill in action, McPadden followed Bill and Michelle's events in Chicago after their Quimby's appearance: "At the Music Box, which is my other main cultural hub in Chicago, Bill and Michelle had a four-film midnight movie series and they showed *Pets, Last House on Dead End Street* on DVD—*thanks a lot*—and a couple of other movies. I went to all of them. I get there and my friend was the manager of the theater, and he just looked at me when I got there, like, 'I'm drowning. I can't deal… "Lizard Man" is a Nightmare.' He called Bill 'Lizard Man…' They got a pretty good crowd for *Pets*. And Michelle does this big intro like *'The legendary… Bill… Landis!'* And like no one really knows who the fuck he is except me and my ten interested friends. So I stand up and I'm cheering, and they had their kid, Baby Sleazoid, who was like a seven year old girl at that point, running around at midnight. I watched them. They looked like they were miserable with each other and miserable with existing."

Bill's increasingly hostile, delusional, and suspicious behavior made it clear that drugs had asserted their influence in his life in a major way again, and this time, while Michelle may defend his professional contributions to cinema journalism, only Bill could save himself—and he was struggling to figure out how to do that.

"I was on the phone with him, and what had happened was my brother had an addiction to painkillers and ultimately did die as a result of them," Keith Crocker recalls of one of his final conversations with Bill. "My brother had a heart attack trying to get off of them. He was trying to withdraw. After that happened, I told Bill, and Bill was sobbing. He was sobbing and he said 'Do you think that's going to happen to me?' I said no Bill, not if you're on top of it, if you're ahead of this it won't happen to you. But he was sobbing because in my brother's death he was foreseeing his own addiction issues and was like, 'I could end up like that.' Yeah, you could, but right now you're alive and you still have options. I remember that phone call clearly. I was moved by it. I was quite taken back. It's indicative of what was going on, that things were wrong, that he was questioning his own ability to fight addiction. That this was a problematic thing. It was something he never beat."

The last months of Bill's life are even more mysterious than the years leading up to them. Records indicate he'd moved into a one-bedroom apartment in

Chicago, but his address is one of the few paper trails he left behind. With Michelle and Victoria gone, he began to isolate himself from his friends; those once closest to him recall a cutting-off of contact, a growing distance. Beginning in the summer of 2008, Bill Landis seemed to have disappeared from the world. The man who'd once stepped onstage in Jim Jones gear to lead worshippers in faux-suicide and who'd regaled Alamo Drafthouse patrons with tales of the Deuce in the bad old days had become a shadow of the limitless source of energy he'd once been. At one point, anger and indignity and the insurmountable pain of being human had been enough fuel for the rampaging fire of life and zeal and hate and love and obsession and intelligence and dedication and truth-seeking and scholarship that was Bill Landis. That was all gone now, though. Maybe it was the drugs; maybe it was losing Michelle and Victoria; maybe it was the awful, crippling weight of all the pain that came with his lived experiences. Only Bill knows; he's in no position to talk now.

Bill Landis died on December 23rd, 2008, two days before Christmas—his favorite holiday, per his friends, a fact attested to by one of the last known photos of him, posing with Art Ettinger in a room decorated with snowmen and other holiday ornaments. He was walking down a street in Chicago when he suddenly tumbled to the pavement; one witness recalled thinking he'd tripped. Another thought he'd lost his balance while trying to tie his shoe. The state of Illinois is protective regarding death inquests for anyone other than immediate family members; a full accounting of the end of his life isn't possible with the available information. What is certain is that he was dead when he hit the sidewalk, felled by a massive heart attack. He was 49. Michelle was summoned to the scene of his demise; as she would later recount in an email to a friend who wishes to remain anonymous: "Bill died. I saw him tonight. Came for him. I am alone here. I saw him go in the black bag." There is no record of his final resting place; the paper trail goes cold after indicating his body may have been returned to Florida for internment by his parents. Those seeking to pay their respects are probably best to make a pilgrimage to his beloved Times Square, however Disneyfied, or take a stroll down 42nd Street.

Or maybe light a candle for him at the Church of the Incarnation.

Bill Landis was both a man of the world and a man who created his own world; our contemporary conception of the Deuce, as it's known both through its depiction in pop culture as well as our broader cultural memory, owes as much to reality as it does to his depiction of it. He codified what "grindhouse" meant a decade before it began to enter the popular lexicon. He laid the groundwork not only for zine culture as it evolved out of the 1980s but the entire current state of genre journalism. Hero worship, blind obedience, and unchecked awe were not words in his vocabulary. Bill didn't give passes for bad behavior or cinematic ineptitude to people who were straight, attractive, and white; he preferred it if they *weren't*, as a matter of fact. He turned an analytical magnifying glass on a subgenre of films whose audiences were too willing to accept them sincerely and uncritically; he documented and preserved a subculture of homosexuals and drug addicts and trans individuals and sex workers and POC at the hour of its death, even as polite society would have rather it shut up and gone quietly into the neon-lit night. He was a pioneer, a trailblazer, a radical.

The fallout from his death was as bifurcated and sensational as Bill's own life. He was given scant, generic eulogies on a few genre sites who only really knew of him through the *Sleazoid* book and spoke of him in vaguely laudatory terms. Elsewhere, the response was more irreverent. Comment sections on articles regarding his death were crammed with anonymous messages from past acquaintances whom he'd burned through harassment and abuse—they were eager to bury, not praise him. McPadden penned a lengthy—and often hilarious— obituary on *Mr. Skin,* recalling his negative experiences while also memorializing Bill's legacy and concluding "I miss him already. And I always will... I love [him] for what he gave the world." Later, he would end our own conversation by elaborating, "This is someone who was possessed of some degree of genius, and as many people with that condition are, he dealt with it through drugs and self-destructive behavior. He seemed lost and miserable. And it's a tragedy to me that he either never got clean or never got to a situation where the drugs didn't interfere with his writing and creativity. With *Sleazoid Express* he did something no one else has ever done, and he did it brilliantly, and he did it better than anyone else has ever done. He was the classic tortured soul. And I'm sorry he was so tortured."

"He did something unique, and it changed over the years and became even more unique. He influenced a lot of people, he wrote about a lot of things that other people didn't," Mike Weldon says.

Greg Goodsell is equally poignant in his summation of Bill's life and destiny: "I would compare him to Diane Arbus. Arbus took her camera to 42nd Street and was similarly inspired by a 42nd Street revival of *Freaks* and started doing her freak photography. There's a classic photo of hers, it's called *Movie on 42nd Street*. Diane Arbus was an anthropologist and Bill was an anthropologist. Diane Arbus told a friend, 'I'm going to photograph evil,' and she succeeded, but she didn't take into consideration that the evil further down the hole is part of the bargain."

"He ultimately succumbed to what he tried to live," Keith Crocker says.

Says Carl Abrahamsson: "It's a shame that he passed so young. He had the kind of quality where you mix your personal experience and history with this beautiful, specifically American journalistic writing. It's very rare. He was a gem. I really loved Bill's writing. It was so passionate; I can't find another word for it. There's something that's so engaging where you have someone who knows a lot about things, in this case the environment and the films themselves. It's written so well, with almost this kind of beatnik panache. I loved that all along, and you compare that with *Gore Gazette* for existence, it doesn't really compare. But Bill was always something else… I'm very, very fond of New Journalism. The New York environment, Gay Talese and all these great writers who were simply *passionate*. And I always felt that Bill had, even in the tiniest reviews, that same kind of quality that was so great because it was written in a very condense, stripped language. It was so to the point. Even people like Dominick Dunne and Gay Talese, they're really great writers in the sense they are always part of the story. It's completely biased in a way, but that's what makes it interesting. The same thing for Bill. Bill had that extra dimension of having been inside the business not only as a projectionist or having to clean up those filthy theaters but also in terms of having been Bobby. There's no beating around the bush that he was the real deal. He knew what he was talking about and he wrote about it in such a wonderful way. At the same time, he could write these things about Dyanne Thorne or even rarer kinds of people giving them the same accolades as though they had been Kim Novak or some big movie star. That kind of quality is completely magical."

A friend who maintained contact with him until the summer of 2008 and who wishes to remain anonymous says he believes there was an element of self-destruction in Bill's end: "He mentioned to me for years he never wanted to grow old."

Art Ettinger—probably the person closest to Bill when he died—mused on how he thought Bill would want to be remembered: "I think he would be flattered by the concept that he was a trailblazer. He was kind of humble about that, but I feel as though he definitely was moved by those of us that would sincerely express to him how influential he was and how much he meant to our developments as writers and viewers. I think that he would like to be remembered as a trailblazer, as a historian, as someone who memorialized 42nd St. And he was really proud of his ability to transition from-- you look at *Sleazoid Express* and how raw it was compared to something like the *Anger* book, published by a mainstream major press, and for him to be published in *The Village Voice* so frequently. I think he would like to be remembered both as a trailblazer and as a serious writer… A rare trailblazer who lived up to his height; he was singularly well-loved and verbal, kind, hilarious, and worthy of his place in history."

Michelle herself was— and remains— publicly silent in the wake of Bill's death, but Jim Morton recalls his own heart-rending final interaction with her: "I wrote to [Michelle] shortly after he died and sent my condolences and all of that. She wrote back and said, 'I miss him every fucking hour of the day.'"

I would like to think that there was a final transcendence for Bill; that, walking the streets of Chicago as the seconds of his life ticked away, he found himself back on his beloved Deuce one last time, in spirit if not in reality, devoid of the pain and suffering of its addicts and refugees but filled with the vibrant life of new movies, new art to be consumed, limitless cinematic possibilities and excitement. I'd like to think that there's at last been a final cleansing, a removal of everything that caused him pain and made him cause pain to others; that, somewhere, in a great grindhouse in the sky, Bill Landis—not Bobby Spector or Joe Monday or Mr. Sleazoid but *Bill*—has a fine balcony seat, and is happy at last as the feature rolls on, and on, and on.

Mr. DJ, please play a song for Bill: "Burnin' for You" by the Blue Oyster Cult, a lullaby for the lost New York he loved so much and taught us all to love, too. For all he gave the world, for all he gave me, and, most importantly, for Bill himself.

Let the movie never end.

APPENDIX

The Fangoria Milligan Interview

Bill Landis' sole piece of writing for Fangoria *magazine was a seminal, in-depth interview with Andy Milligan, which ran in Volume 1, Issue 20, dated July 1982. Coming out firmly in the middle of* Sleazoid's *initial run, it was many* Fango *readers' introduction to the films of Milligan and nearly presented an opportunity for Landis to take his writing and* Sleazoid Express *into the mainstream. As a result of Landis' subsequent attempts to review queer cinema in the pages of the magazine, then-editor Bob Martin had Landis blacklisted from ever writing for the publication again amidst homophobic claims that he promoted child pornography. Now, almost forty years later, the current owners of* Fangoria *have kindly consented to allow Landis' work to be reprinted here for educational purposes and to help further preserve his legacy. Tremendous thanks to Tara Ainsley, Abhi Goel and Phil Nobile Jr. for opening up the* Fangoria *vault and allowing a piece of Bill's writing to live again.*

Milligan! Andy Milligan, Ground-Breaking Goremeister from the 60's, Tells His Story

By Bill Landis

Editor's Note: In answer to popular demand (from Douglas A. Roy, 19 Standard Ave., West Warwick, RI), we are proud to present this in-depth one-part interview with the director of Bloodthirsty Butchers, *Staten Island's answer to Herschel Gordon Lewis—the indefatigable Andy Milligan. The man who tackled this task, the only man for the job, was Bill Landis, gore and sleaze expert extraordinaire, and publisher of* Sleazoid Express, *a monthly tabloid-format newsletter which is the most complete guide on horror and exploitation films. Subscriptions are $10 per year. The address: Sleazoid, Dept. S, 8033. Sunset Blvd., Suite 824, Los Angeles, CA 90046.*

Along with Herschell Gordon Lewis, with whom FANGORIA readers are already well acquainted, one of the most active filmmakers to emerge in the 1960's who consistently churned out gore movies was Andy Milligan. Like Lewis, Milligan was extraordinarily prolific, completing 23 features to date. However, Milligan's movies were made on budgets that would have frustrated even the extremely frugal Lewis. Milligan's cinematic terrain essentially included gore horror and exploitation films. The latter, like *Kiss Me, Kiss Me, Kiss Me; Guttertrash;* and *The Filthy Five* included language and sexual situations that were considered, in the 1960's, to be daring. His horror films possess a unifying style, making them immediately recognizable as his—period piece settings; a homemade feel in terms of costumes and production values; sometimes grainy, 16mm blowup photography; plots so thin and yet convoluted that they can be summarized in either a sentence or in pages; violence ranging from graphic to obviously fake; utilization of horror movie icons like mad priests, vampires, werewolves and hunchbacks; and finally, elements of camp humor. Milligan shot many of his horror films in the somewhat suburban New York City borough of Staten Island; many were released by veteran New York City exploitation distributor William Mishkin. Unlike many of Lewis' films, Milligan's still turn up at drive-ins and grind houses, and he currently operates an off-Broadway theater. He came across as being highly intelligent, personable, serious about his art, and as individualistic as his movies.

Fang: How did you get into movies?

AM: I was in the dress business. There was Art Ford, who was a disc jockey. I happened to know he was into films and so I asked him what I should start out with if I wanted to get into films. He told me about an Auricon, which was a single system camera, 16mm, so I purchased one for about $700, $800 at the time. It was an optical sound camera, which is not the best. Over a four month period I put together a film, shooting weekends, called *Liz*. I called different distributors in the phone book, many of them. I had a screening of it at the Player's Theater on Mac-Dougal Street. Out of maybe 30 phone calls, four showed up. One of them was Bill Mishkin. They liked the film, Bill especially, but he said that, for his market, he had to have more nudity, breast shots, whatever, in it, for it to be more commercial. I didn't pay any attention to him. I put out another call, had another screening and a handful showed up. They weren't that interested, especially in 16mm. At that time, they didn't do many blowups in New York. So, Mishkin came again and I told him I'd do the four extra scenes, which were like thirty, forty seconds of models in the dressing room and that sort of thing. He opened it at the World Theater and it ran for 29 weeks as *The Promiscuous Sex*. I owned 50% of the film, and, by the time the distributor does his own packaging, you're knocked down to 25% ownership. I ended up with this so-called 25%. I sat around for two or three months looking to see some return from the film and on paper it looked like it'd be years before anything came through. So he offered me money to do another film—whatever I wanted to do. I had a witch thing that I wanted to shoot down in New Jersey with my cast and so forth, so we went down there. I shot this in about eight or nine days in Manasquan, New Jersey. We shot the whole thing down there. It's called *The Naked Temptress* or *The Naked Witch*. That did very well. Then, at the time I was editing that, there were these filmmakers called ASA, Abrams, Seigal and I forgot the third person. They had seen me working on a moviola at Camera Mart, which used to be around Lincoln Center Square at the time. They had just made a film for a character called Jerry Balsam —JER Pictures. They had made a film for him, which I didn't know about at the time, for about 460,000 or 580,000. I told them I made mine for about $9500. They immediately signed me for a three picture deal with ASA. So I made the three pictures, called *Depraved, The Degenerates,* and *The Ghastly Ones. Depraved* was an after-the-atomic-war thing shot in Woodstock in about six or seven days. *The Degenerates* was shot in New York. The Ghastly Ones was a horror film we shot out in Staten Island in a Victorian setting in a house that, at the time, I owned. I finished the films and I was supposed to have gotten returns, so I asked to see the books. Turns out that they were into hock to this Balsam character up to their necks. I took it to my lawyer, we tried to sue. It turned out I was the third party and there was no way I could touch Mr. Balsam. He knew this, and sat in my lawyer's office and said, "Yeah, I'll make $80,000 off the films, each one of them, but fuck Andy. You want $3,000, I'll give you $3,000, that's it." So my lawyer advised me and we settled for the $3,000. Just remember—stay away from Mr. Balsam.

Fang: *The Ghastly Ones* was the first film you made in your Victorian horror mode, filmed on Staten Island.

AM: The reason I did mostly period stuff is because most things are retitled and sent out again and again. Let's say you do a mini-skirt, you're limited within a two year period. Whereas, if you do a costume setting, it can be reissued and reissued and reissued and you can't tell what year it was made. Just like Hammer Films, they're all in costume, in a period. You really can't remember what year they were made unless you're an aficionado like this character here that's interviewing me.

Fang: Is there anything particular about horror movies that interested you which drove you to make them?

AM: I think all kids that go into filmmaking were moved by horror films when they were kids. The fascination of them.

Fang: Any particular ones you were moved by?

AM: *The Thing*. By today's standards—*The Texas Chainsaw Massacre* is the best one. The acting's not great, but the effects are the granddaddy of all before they started getting all the gimmicks. Now they publicize the gimmicks too much, so that you can't be scared because you're looking for the way it's done. The real mystique is missing from films today, which is wrong. It should be kept secret, it should not have releases. In fact, when you're doing something, keep it quiet, don't send out releases, just explode the bomb when it opens. Don't send out press and all that. This is advice to young filmmakers.

Fang: After *The Ghastly Ones*, you began making more

horror movies for Mishkin.

AM: There was a Leslie Elliot who had Cinemania Films in London and they had seen quite a few of my films. They booked them, I guess, through Mishkin. Mishkin wouldn't introduce me to them, but Jerry Balsam had. This Leslie Elliot. They signed me for three pictures a year for five years; I made two pictures, *Nightbirds,* in black and white, and a horror film called *The Body Beneath.* The father stepped back in the business at the time. He and the father fought, threw the son out and defaulted on my contract. I sat around for months waiting for it to be settled. In the meantime I made two or three more films for Mishkin in 16mm in London. In London there's no freedom of expression like there is here. They won't rent equipment to you unless you belong to a studio. I had all my own equipment, luckily, and could go right through customs with my 16mm. Otherwise, you wouldn't be able to do anything in England without having work permits. It's not a free country like it is here. America's the only place where you can do what you want. I made two more films, the Sweeney Todd thing, which was *Bloodthirsty Butchers,* and *Curse of the Full Moon,* which was the original title before it was turned into *The Rats Are Coming, The Werewolves Are Here.* The reason why it was called *The Rats Are Coming, The Werewolves Are Here* is because, at the time, *Willard* came out and rats were the big thing. He [Mishkin] decided that we were going to shoot some extra scenes here in New York and we shot the rat scenes. The rat scenes were shot in Staten

Island, with Hope Stansbury, and the rat salesman, and so forth, with his head chewed off. The outcome of the disagreement between the father and son on the business was that I brought the two films back here. I started my own company, called Nova. *Guru, the Mad Monk* was made under that Nova. We made *Guru* in six days. It's the shortest film of all. My first double system, 35mm. I didn't know about sync sound, so I had to sync up the whole thing by putting slugs of film in order to match the sound with the picture. So I spent a lot of work putting that thing together.

Fang: What do you think of the violence in movies like *Bloodthirsty Butchers*? Did you do it deliberately to be commercial?

AM: Yes, well, that's the whole thing. See, to make a suspense film, it doesn't carry today's standards, very few people like suspense films. You have to have production values to make a suspense film. You don't have to have as many production values—you can do a low budget with horror and blood and guts and all that sort of stuff. It's easier to make bloody stuff and it's going to make more money by today's audiences than a suspense film. A suspense film is fine, but you need a lot of gloss, excellent acting, excellent storyline. A horror film —you don't need a storyline. I think you should have one, but most of the junk that comes out is no storyline. The acting doesn't have to be sterling as long as it's bloody.

Fang: Some people go to low budget movies because of the unintended laughs due to the amateurish performances.

AM: When you're making a film, you don't think about anything but getting the damn thing finished within the budget. The highest budget I've ever had was $20,000; the lowest was $7,500 (for *The Naked Witch* and *The Promiscuous Sex*), including the blowup in those days. I was the first one to have four-letter words in films. Also, the first nudity, I think, frontal, male and female. Not that it's a criterion, it's just the idea that if you used the word "fuck" in those days you were X-rated automatically. It had nothing to do with nudity or sex.

Fang: Did you use four-letter words in the horror films?

AM: No, because they're usually period pieces. I designed and made all the costumes on every one of them. We had a crew of five—I never had more than five people on a set ever. All the credits you see on my films are all made up names. I usually had the same kids. Haal Borske was always helping me, the Borske brothers, John and Haal. You don't need more than five people—if you have more than five people, they're under your feet and they're a pain in the ass. If the producer wants a bloody horror film, they usually don't care what period it's in or where it's shot, at a resort or in an old hotel. They don't care, as long as you can turn over their cheap dollar into $400.

Fang: Any memorable incidents while making movies?

AM: Oh, being hung by my feet by two people I trusted during *Kiss Me, Kiss Me, Kiss Me*. Two guys holding me by my feet from a roof of a building six stories up to get that shot down on the Street. That I'll never do again now, of course, but when you're young you're crazy. As you get older you get crazier but more cautious. I enjoyed doing *Nightbirds* —which has never been released—because it was shot four doors down from the third victim of Jack the Ripper on Commercial Street in the backyard there. You can see Petticoat Lane in the distance. We were thrown out of Highgate Cemetery for being without a permit in *The Body Beneath*. We had to go around and sneak in the back way. One of us detained the caretaker while the rest of us were shooting. We had to make up names—we bluffed our way into shooting in Highgate Cemetery, which is one of the most gorgeous cemeteries, I think, in the world. Setting Haal Borske, each time, on fire—he's such a delight to set on fire. The eating of the rabbit —he practically threw up. We had a dead rabbit and a live rabbit in *The Ghastly Ones*. He supposedly kills the live one—the dead one's a little rancid, we had it for about three days. He had to put his mouth right on its stomach and practically threw up on it.

Fang: Your films were done so low budget that most people couldn't make them on those budgets, even then.

AM: Well, that's because I wrote my own scripts, did

my own camera work, did my own stills, fitted all my own costumes and did all the sets, basically, with one or two people helping me. One person could basically do all the stuff. It wasn't ego, it was necessity. There was no money. Mishkin is a cheap, cheap, cheap, cheap man.

Fang: When you began doing horror films in the 60s and early 70s, there was only Herschel! Gordon Lewis consistently doing gore horror, along with George Romero later. Did they have any impact on you?

AM: No, I don't even know them. I don't know anyone today. I'm a loner. I don't believe in bumping noses with other filmmakers. I don't even know those names till today. I was grinding out three, four films a year. I didn't have time to worry about who anyone else was. I don't like to show up at a cocktail party saying I'm a filmmaker. I think it's shit for young filmmakers to do this. Stick to yourself; stick to your own guns; keep everything quiet; keep everything private. Everyone steals ideas and things like that and you have to be very, very private in what you do. You don't need your name in press releases; all you need is it on the screen.

Fang: What about filming in Staten Island?

AM: Staten Island has all the elements for anyplace you want to shoot in the world. It's got the seacoast of England; it has the south of France up in Grimes Mill; it has waterfronts; it has seaports; they shoot all the Irish

Spring commercials out there—it has the Ireland country stuff; it has houses; it has carriages. It has everything you need out there.

Fang: In terms of overall impact, which one of your films is your favorite?

AM: I don't have a favorite film; the only film I have is the ones I'm working on.

Fang: Which one is that?

AM: *The House of the Seven Belles.* It hasn't been mixed yet. It's an antebellum horror film. It's the Old South—the *Gone With the Wind* period. It's seven belles, seven girls, without a father or mother and how they survive in the Old South. It's quite lush. It's overly long; it's two-and-a-half hours already and I have to cut it way down.

Fang: Was that shot in Staten Island also?

AM: It was practically all shot In Staten Island. And it looks exactly like the Old South. The costumes are gorgeous. It's one of my best films, actually, I think, production-wise. So far there's been about $12,000 spent on it.

Fang: Do you believe in cinéma vérité?

AM: Cinéma vérité. All my films were accused of being

cinéma vérité and every one of them we rehearsed heavily. There wasn't one moment of improvisation. Most filmmakers don't know anything about actors. They come out of film school—film schools are the most dangerous things in the world. They teach you to overspend, be too slow, be pedantic, think too tight. Film schools—they're all over the place—are the worst things in the world. Just get a camera and go out and shoot, you'll learn more that way than you'll learn from a school. Same thing about acting. Acting schools are dangerous. Get out and act. You don't learn anything in school. They teach you the $7,000,000 production.

Fang: How about some of the more memorable moments in your horror films, like the throat-slitting in *Bloodthirsty Butchers*?

AM: I don't know if that's in the prints anymore. He [Mishkin] cut so much of the blood out. One of my best scenes in *Bloodthirsty Butchers* is the chopping up of the body—cutting the legs. I don't know if that's in there anymore. These prints have been butchered so much by Mishkin and his idiot son. When you've done 23 features, you don't remember too much.

Fang: What kind of gore scenes do you find easiest to shoot?

AM: They're all too much work. There isn't anything you can do today without doing all this. Fake bodies and heads and all this stuff you can do. I never had any of this stuff. My stuff was always plain clay, flesh color painted, chicken guts, the fundamentals that I could buy at any store anywhere. It would take you half a day to rig six seconds on the screen. Remember these were low budget. And only because I had a very cheap producer [Mishkin]. Later on, typical of cheap producers, they'll accuse you of no production values when they haven't given you money to do any. Just remember, probably the highest budget on the Mishkin horror films was $13,500, including the budget on the blowup. On the double system ones, the highest budget is $20,000. *Blood!* Is a good one. That's the one Bryanston had. That was shot in about 10 days. It's got the son of Lawrence Talbot, the werewolf, and the daughter of Dracula, the vampire. They've had an arranged marriage. It takes place about 1894, 1895. Victorian—Edwardian, actually. They move to Staten Island. They come in a boat and they've got this little retarded dwarf sort of woman who they bleed regularly for her blood; retarded because there's no oxygen going to her brain. Talbot has signed for this house and he gets rid of the landlord immediately, runs to the back door, throws open the door and they come running in with this body all wrapped up, steaming. All of a sudden he throws off the blankets and there's this wrinkled, old, mummified body. He pumps blood into her and the next scene is this gorgeous wife of his, which is the vampire, sitting on the back step with the sunshade over her so the sun can't get at her. She's a very jealous shrew of a wife. The only thing that brings on his werewolfism is when he gets extremely angry, so they have to keep him pacified all the time so he won't get angry and turn into a werewolf. Of course, whenever she gets carried away—at night, she can't sleep and she can't take the sun at all. It's watered down versions of Dracula and the werewolf. It's a domestic wrangle. It's quite lovely. It's got all sorts of crazy stuff in it. They've got a chemical lab and they're always working in the lab. And the guy and the gal are in love, the two assistants. He's dying and she's dying with a growth on her leg.

Fang: How do you feel about people taking your horror films as comedies?

AM: We didn't make them as comedies, but, when you have no money, that'll lead to the laughable part of it. I don't care one way or the other. At the time they came out people didn't laugh. They don't realize the low budget they were made on. I'd like to see people match the budget anytime, anywhere, at any time in history.

Fang: Anything else you'd like to add about contemporary movies?

AM: ... Film, of course, will be out in another 40 years. It'll all be video. Why should we be worried about celluloid and developing and all that crap when we have video. Film will be extinct in another 40 or 50 years, except in the archives. Remember that. This will be before we hit the year 2020 or 2040. There won't be such a thing as film; it'll be extinct. It won't be called filmmaking, it'll be called picturemaking or whatever. It'll look the same and people won't know the difference.

A Guide to Milligan Horror

The Naked Witch (1964)—A college student falls under the spell of a witch executed in the 1800's.
The Degenerates (1967)—Post atomic war survivors in the year 2000.
The Ghastly Ones (1968)—Murders over an inheritance via hanging. Disembowelment, a pitchfork and an axe.
Bloodthirsty Butchers (1970)—The Sweeney Todd story, complete with throat slittings, dismemberment and a woman's breast in a meat pie.
Guru, the Mad Monk (1970)—The demented doings of schizophrenic Father Guru, a prison chaplain in Central Europe circa 1480.
The Body Beneath (1970)—British vampires emigrate to America.
Torture Dungeon (1970)—Murders over a throne in olde England.
The Rats Are Coming, The Werewolves Are Here (1971)—A lycanthropic family, with rat footage later added.
Legacy of Blood (1972)—More inheritance murders along the lines of The Ghastly Ones.
Blood! (1973)—The marriage between Dracula's daughter and Lawrence Talbot's son.

Acknowledgments

Thanks as always to my wife, Kayleigh, who's gone on the whole Bill journey with me. It was with her encouragement and inspiration I first embarked on telling Bill's story in 2018, and through the disastrous COVID summer of 2020 it was our in-depth discussions about Bill's life and character during daily walks in the park that helped me figure out a way to assemble this book. She helped me bring what's essentially been a 17-year journey to what I feel is a satisfying conclusion and I'll be forever indebted to her for that and so much more.

Thanks to my parents for their continued love and support despite the fact their son writes about sleazy porn stars for a living.

Thanks to my brother, Brian, who's always there for me; he was the first person I ever introduced to Bill's writing. Memories of our laying on the living room floor, reading aloud from the *Sleazoid* book and nearly pissing ourselves laughing, are some of my happiest from a turbulent time in my life.

Thanks to Anya Stanley, who transcribed all of the interviews excerpted in this book. Anya's diligence allowed me to focus on telling Bill's story and tracking down more leads and seriously expedited my work.

Thanks to Mike Vanderbilt, who indirectly set me down the road to writing this book. He was the one who introduced me to The Daily Grindhouse when we first met at Fantastic Fest 2015, and had he not placed that button in my hand I might never have found a home for the article that eventually grew into this book.

Thanks to everyone who agreed to be interviewed for this book, including, in no particular order, Art Ettinger, Jim Morton, Kurt Loder, Keith Crocker, Greg Goodsell, Gary Hertz, Michael J. Weldon, Carl Abrahamsson, and other friends of Bill's who wish to remain anonymous. With so many of Bill's acquaintances dead or in the wind, their contributions were invaluable in telling his story.

A special thanks to "Mad" Ron Roccia not only for his time but also his providing me with several back issues of *Sleazoid*, including the seminal *Zeppelin* issue.

A very special thanks to Mike "McBeardo" McPadden, whom I interviewed only two months before his own death and who was slated to contribute more memories to this book at the time of his passing. His insight into Bill's final years was invaluable and his impressions of Bill gut-bustingly hilarious.

Thanks to Aaron W. Graham for providing me with some back issues of *Sleazoid* I was missing, as well as copies of some of Bill's- *ahem*- "adult features" for research purposes.

Thanks to Jason Alvino for his friendship and the contribution of his encyclopedic knowledge of New York geography to this project.

RIP to Jacob "The Nord" Hacker, who was also there with me during my initial teenage fascination with Bill and who was a very Bill-like personality himself. You are loved, and you are missed.

Thanks to Mark Miller for his ongoing belief in me as a writer and willingness to publish this.

Thanks too to my Daily Grindhouse compatriots Jon Abrams, Mary Beth McAndrews, Katelyn Nelson, and Andrew Allan, who provided me with my initial platform to tell Bill's story and who encouraged me to expand it into its current form.

About the Author

Preston Fassel is an award-winning writer whose work has appeared in *FANGORIA, Rue Morgue, Screem,* and on The Daily Grindhouse, Dread Central, and Cinedump.com. He is the author of the first published biography of British horror actress Vanessa Howard, *Remembering Vanessa,* which appeared in the Spring 2014 issue of Screem. His debut novel, *Our Lady of the Inferno,* won the 2019 Independent Publisher's Gold Medal for Horror and was named one of the ten best books of the year by Bloody Disgusting.

CPSIA information can be obtained
at www.ICGtesting.com
Printed in the USA
LVHW050856171121
703498LV00002B/3